Better Homes and Gardens®

Home Building

Idea File

Better Homes and Gardens® Books
Des Moines, Iowa

Better Homes and Gardens® Books
An imprint of Meredith® Books

Home Building Idea File
Editor: Brian Kramer
Contributing Editors: Cynthia Pearson, Dan Weeks
Art Director: David Jordan
Copy Chief: Terri Fredrickson
Copy and Production Editor: Victoria Forlini
Editorial Operations Manager: Karen Schirm
Managers, Book Production: Pam Kvitne, Marjorie J. Schenkelberg, Rick von Holdt
Contributing Copy Editor: Kim Catanzarite
Contributing Proofreaders: Margaret Smith, Becky Etchen, Sue Fetters
Contributing Illustrator: Tom Stocki
Indexer: Beverly A. Nightenhelser
Editorial and Design Assistants: Kaye Chabot, Karen McFadden, Mary Lee Gavin

Meredith® Books
Editor in Chief: Linda Raglan Cunningham
Design Director: Matt Strelecki
Executive Editor, Home Decorating and Design: Denise L. Caringer

Publisher: James D. Blume
Executive Director, Marketing: Jeffrey Myers
Executive Director, New Business Development: Todd M. Davis
Executive Director, Sales: Ken Zagor
Director, Operations: George A. Susral
Director, Production: Douglas M. Johnston
Business Director: Jim Leonard

Vice President and General Manager: Douglas J. Guendel

Better Homes and Gardens® Magazine
Editor in Chief: Karol DeWulf Nickell

Meredith Publishing Group
President, Publishing Group: Stephen M. Lacy
Vice President-Publishing Director: Bob Mate

Meredith Corporation
Chairman and Chief Executive Officer: William T. Kerr

In Memoriam: E. T. Meredith III (1933–2003)

All of us at Better Homes and Gardens® Books are dedicated to providing you with information and ideas to enhance your home. We welcome your comments and suggestions. Write to us at: Better Homes and Gardens Books, Home Decorating and Design Editorial Department, 1716 Locust St., Des Moines, IA 50309-3023.

If you would like to purchase any of our home decorating and design, cooking, crafts, gardening, or home improvement books, check wherever quality books are sold. Or visit us at: bhgbooks.com

Inspiring Case Studies to Plan Your New Home

Welcome to *Better Homes and Gardens®*

Home Building Idea File, the best investment you'll make in creating a new home that suits your needs, budget, lifestyle, and taste.

For starters, the book sparks your imagination with a style gallery of the most popular styles. You'll find a wide range of styles—including Greek Revival and Georgian, nostalgic farmhouses and Arts and Crafts bungalows, high-style International and contemporary designs—and discussions of the advantages and limitations of each.

A chapter on design and location helps you prioritize your housing needs—and identify what type of neighborhood suits you and the kind of lot you'd like to build on.

The heart of the book walks you through several case studies of achievable world-class new homes with tips, strategies, and information that will help you customize your project to suit your needs and lifestyle. Sidebars and tip boxes highlight and explain ideas you can adapt to your own home. Idea File sections feature techniques, materials, and information that will make your project shine.

The final chapter helps you refine your dreams into a plan that results in a home that meets your needs now and in the future. Topics include energy conservation techniques, options for getting your home designed and built, universal design considerations, and use of the latest green building materials and technologies.

Style
Gallery

Vivacious Victorian

• **Victorian Gothic homes feature porches, turrets, and filigrees that are romantic in nature and rich in detail.**

This eye-catching, architect-designed Victorian Gothic house on the Connecticut coast is a study in how this exuberant vintage style can be reinterpreted to blend old-fashioned panache with contemporary livability. Its open, airy floor plan features wide open views and lots of natural light.

To avoid dominating the streetscape, this four-story house is sited farther back on the lot than its smaller, simpler neighbors. The house wears a pale yellow coat of paint with white trim—far more subdued than the traditional bright pinks, purples, and greens typical of historical Victorian "painted ladies."

Siting the house back from the street made fancier architectural aspects possible. On the exterior, the architect reinterpreted Victorian details to include Moroccan onion-shape window heads, wave-pattern shingles, star medallions, and two turrets. Those details add to the home's appeal—and because Victo-rians mixed and matched styles, they blend well with the house.

To get the most living space from a narrow waterfront site, the plans called for four levels. Because the property slopes up from the street, then falls downward toward the water, the main floor is one floor above street level. The first floor, which is below ground on the street side and at walk-out level on the water side, makes for an easily accessible living area.

Inside, the home combines period detailing and nostalgic room shapes. The main level features a great-room layout with a living and dining room combination that offers plenty of space for family gatherings.

A widow's walk, or turret room, adjoins the attic on the top floor and offers spectacular, tree-top level views of the water. The attic is used as guest space. An L-shape master suite includes a circular space below the widow's walk. The suite also includes a vestibule and walk-in cedar closet.

In executing a project that melds old-fashioned architecture with a modern floor plan, it helps to have a project team that includes an

Style Notes

Popular from about 1860 to 1900, Victorian designs took inspiration from newly available mass-produced trim work to create ornate yet affordable homes for the middle class. In contrast to the simple, symmetrical, classically based styles that preceded it, Victorian houses featured steeply pitched roofs, asymmetrical floor plans, and multitextured and multicolor exterior walls. The Victorian era's romance with the past encouraged the incorporation of stylistic elements of remote lands, and mass production made such elaborate detailing affordable. The result is a style that is varied and exuberant, exotic and eclectic, one that incorporates elements from sources as diverse as Swiss cottages, French mansions, East-Indian minarets, half-timbered English country houses, and Italian villas.

1 *Typical of Victorian houses, this home's exterior textures are varied and eclectic. Tidal-washed cobblestone was used on the foundation wall. Carriage-style garage doors, wave-pattern shingles, and brackets, filigree, and detailing give the house a rich and fanciful texture. A roll-down canopy shades the terraced seating area.*

2 *Because you can see the house from the water, special attention was paid to the rear elevation. Many windows add texture and detail while providing waterfront views from almost every room.*

3 *Large windows in the living room and the adjacent dining alcove overlook boats at anchor. French doors from the alcove lead to a terrace beyond, allowing alfresco dining.*

4 *An open floor plan results in casual, light-filled living spaces. The fireplace surround's cresting waves reflect the coastal location.*

5 *The "god of the winds" from an 18th-century map inspired the entryway glass.*

interior designer who will work hand in hand with the architect.

Such a collaboration ensures that the eccentrically shaped rooms that give the plan much of its magnetism are practical as well as whimsical. Here dimensions were carefully planned to allow for sensible furniture arrangements and smooth, unobstructed traffic flow while preserving the interior's vintage feel.

Bringing in an interior designer is also helpful if you have a collection of furniture you'd like to keep. A designer can ensure that those pieces have an appropriate place in your new home.

1

2

These days Victorian architecture is more likely to be suggested than duplicated because much of the mass-produced detailing that gave the original houses texture and allure is no longer available. Today a little ornament goes a long way. You can effectively suggest Victorian style with such details as:

• Turrets or octagonal-shape rooms
• Varied siding patterns, including shingles, clapboard, and "fish scales," and shingles with rounded bottom edges
• Gabled roofs with dormers
• Varied colors on exterior walls, trim, and other architectural details

3

Main Level

Second Level

Third Level

1 A home office adjacent to the kitchen incorporates two workstation areas and a window seat for visitors.

2 The kitchen is open to the living area and retains an old-fashioned feel with cut-glass cabinet pulls, beaded-board cabinet fronts with antiqued paint treatment, and leaded-glass windows.

3 Simple and airy, the master bath features a leaded-glass pocket door and Victorian-style claw-foot tub and fixtures.

4 The widow's walk turret room adds character to the house roofline. Inside, treetop views and a wrap-around window seat make this a favorite play space and observatory.

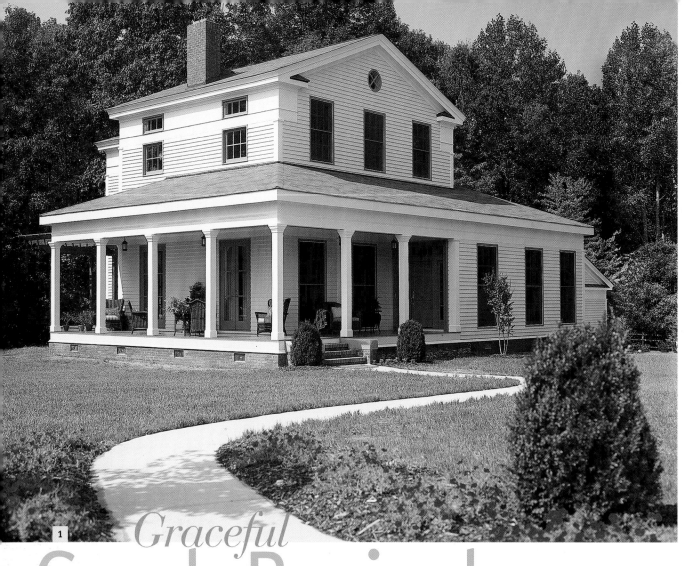

Graceful
Greek Revival

3,000 sq.ft.

FEATURES

• This Greek Revival home has it all: a gracious entry, formal living and dining rooms, through-views, large windows, a wraparound porch, a skylit kitchen, and a deck, patio, and pergola.

• The home was designed by architect Thomas Gordon Smith, former chair of the school of Architecture, Notre Dame University, and one of the world's foremost authorities on Grecian architecture.

If you're looking for a nostalgic style that easily accommodates contemporary life, Greek Revival deserves enthusiastic consideration. The United States' first and most popular national style, Greek Revival remains an American favorite for its simple-yet-elegant classical proportions and its remarkable flexibility.

Vintage homes of this design are found throughout the Northeast, Southeast, and eastern Midwest. Incarnations range from informal farmhouses like this one to grand columned plantation estates.

Enriched with moldings and columns, the style avoids the excess exterior ornamentation that makes some Victorian houses, for example, hard to maintain. The style works

Style Notes

By the 1800s, Americans were tired of following European fashions and ready to forge an architectural style that reflected their own political and philosophical ideals. In ancient Greece, the world's first democracy, Americans found inspiration for the first U.S. building style. Used for both public edifices and humble farmhouses, Grecian buildings were immensely popular between 1820 and 1860. Characterized by classical forms, proportions, and ornamentation, they generally featured a columned facade and a shallow-pitched roof. More formal examples used elaborate columns supporting a pediment over a centered entrance; less formal examples, such as this home, faced the gable end toward the street and emphasized the roofline with cornice moldings and cornice returns. Many grand Greek Revival houses were painted white to symbolize purity. Public buildings often were constructed of marble or limestone for the same reason. More modest residences adapted the style to smaller budgets and local building materials, such as wood lap siding, brick, or fieldstone. Such houses remain among the most handsome structures on the American landscape.

1 *Greek Revival details include a low-pitched roof, a frieze (the horizontal band just below the eaves) that is punctuated with transom windows, a columned porch, and a balanced facade. Angled house placement and a winding path are welcomingly informal variations on the style.*

2 *French doors to the living room make the long leg of the deep, shaded porch a convenient outdoor living area for the whole family.*

3 *In a twist on tradition, the sidelit front entry faces the porch rather than the street, easing the transition from outside to in. Inside, an oak stairway curves to meet the entry, slightly off-center to showcase the banister and newel.*

4 *Every opening frames a view. The doorway to the living room looks through the foyer and an arched passage under the stairway into the dining room.*

5 *It's all in the proportions: Tall windows and French doors, 12-foot ceilings, and a fireplace add up to an old-house feel in the living room.*

1

well with porches, porticos, and pergolas, which invite indoor-outdoor dining, relaxing, and entertaining.

Inside, Greek Revival houses are often bright, thanks to large windows and white, light-reflecting molding and high ceilings. Such interiors provide a restful, gallerylike backdrop that harmonizes with a wide range of furniture styles, from colonial to Mission to modern.

This particular new home, in Greensboro, North Carolina, was inspired by a 19th-century Greek Revival farmhouse in Michigan. With its wraparound porch, gable-end facade, and side-facing front door, it offers an informal twist on the style. Yet it retains all the gracious touches that made this distinctive style so remarkable and enduringly popular, including a

columned porch, a front door embellished with sidelights and transom, narrow lap siding, six-over-six double-hung windows, and a shallow pitched roof with generous cornice moldings. A flat frieze band sporting clerestory windows runs around the top of the second floor—another hallmark of the style.

Inside, a formal plan follows that found in many traditional house styles. Guests are greeted in a foyer with main staircase and powder room. (In this house, the foyer soars two stories high, creating a grand light-filled entrance.) Public areas occupy the front of the house, with a living room to the left and a dining room to the right. The more private areas—a kitchen and master suite—inhabit the rear of the house.

This house shows how adaptable even the most traditional style can be. The large skylit kitchen with island, breakfast nook, and adjoining deck accommodate family activities, informal gatherings, and indoor-outdoor entertaining as well as food preparation. A deck off the kitchen is ideal for family cookouts.

Large windows throughout the house and several through-views result in interiors that are as light and spacious feeling as most contemporary plans. The wraparound porch, accessed from the living room via two sets of French doors, is a constant invitation to step out into the open air. The spacious, comfortable master suite in the rear of the house offers quiet and privacy, plus the luxury of its own pergola-shaded patio.

Upstairs, two more bedrooms fill out the front of the house. The rear of the plan features a useful bonus room that residents can outfit as a fourth bedroom, a family room, or a home office, depending on the needs of the family.

2

Main Level

Upper Level

1 At 10 feet high, the dining room ceiling contributes to an intimate setting.

2 Easy traffic circulation and a variety of long views characterize this house plan, as do such modern amenities as a big kitchen, luxurious master suite, two-story foyer, and four convenient baths.

3 A skylight bathes the kitchen in daylight. A downdraft cooktop and generous counter and storage space make the island a well-placed workstation. Farmhouse allure surrounds the cook, including an apron-front sink, blue and white tile backsplash, and natural maple cabinets with muntined-glass fronts.

4 The laundry room has cabinets, a big sink, and a location near the back door that makes the space ideal for potting plants or cleaning up after yard work.

5 An architect-designed bench forms a comfy spot for serving morning tea to drop-in visitors.

6 A pergola-shaded deck creates an intimate outdoor living space off the master bedroom.

13

1

Just Wrightian

2

F E A T U R E S

• **A low, site-hugging profile belies this home's expansive views. An open floor plan allows every room in the house to take advantage of the vista, yet a clever design preserves a sense of intimacy and privacy too. Natural materials—including 100 tons of stone—integrate the house with its site.**

This gem of a Wrightian house began with a quest to situate a two-story house on a small wedge-shape lot without obstructing the neighbor's view. A flat roof offered a solution, and from there evolved the low-slung home with strong horizontal lines and natural materials that blend into the site. The result borrows much from Frank Lloyd Wright's masterpiece, Fallingwater, in Mill Run, Pennsylvania—and fittingly so, as both homes seem to at once hug the natural landscape and hover over a view of water. In this

1 *Nestled comfortably into a wedge-shape lot, this home is a study in horizontal lines, from its handpicked ledger stone to overlapping rooflines.*

2 *A main-level patio features a flagstone dining area with a pass-through window to the kitchen that encourages outdoor dining and entertaining. A more private deck overlooks the patio.*

3 *The custom-designed entry door leads into the home's anchoring center hall. The space opens onto the dining room and the stairways at the far end of the house, which lead up one level to the guest bedroom and down to the garage. A separate stairway to the right of the entry (not shown) leads to the master bedroom level. To keep the home bright and uncluttered, light fixtures are hidden behind a valance that rims the ceiling.*

4 *Patio doors and a oversize tropical fish aquarium frame the dining room. A built-in maple cabinet and buffet provide storage and serving and display surfaces.*

Style Notes

The style of this home is named for Frank Lloyd Wright, the most famous American architect. Wright single-handedly invented the style in the 1930s and went on to design 50 of these houses before his death in 1959. Since then, other architects have emulated his style and adapted it to the unique demands of a variety of settings. Wrightian houses are instantly recognizable by their strong geometric shapes, overlapping flat or low-pitched roofs (often cantilevered over patios, walkways, or the surrounding landscape), extensive parapeted railings built up of overlapping boards, and lavish use of glass, stone, and brick. Wright's work includes the low-hipped roofs of his Prairie-style homes in the Midwest, the nautilus-shell shape of the Guggenheim Museum in New York City, the gridlike exterior walls of his concrete "textile-block" houses in California, and the serenity of Fallingwater, a celebrated home built over a Pennsylvania stream. Some sources call Fallingwater the most recognized residence of someone not of royal blood in the world. Of all Wright's work, it is Fallingwater's style that the house shown here most closely emulates.

Wright was a demanding architect, prescribing not only every detail of the house but also the manner in which people should live in his creations. Garages and basements were not included in Wright's original designs (though this example integrates a garage seamlessly into its design). Hearths were the spiritual center of the home. Floor plans were open. Furniture was often built-in or designed by the architect himself. A number of stories tell of the architect rearranging furniture when visiting homes he had designed. Charming and charismatic, he could be outright dismissive of clients' concerns. For example, he once told a client who complained about a leaky roof, "That's what happens when you leave a work of art out in the rain."

case, the house also offers a delightful counterpoint to the stately Torrey pines native to the area.

The house presents expansive views from a once-confining site. Its open floor plan allows the rooms to share exterior views—inviting in a sense of limitless light and space while offering privacy. From the entry foyer, the home's public spaces are just a few steps away and the living room, dining room, kitchen, and den flow together.

This home's living room and den flank the public spaces, and each features a striking fireplace of ledger stone—a material that emphasizes the home's typically Wrightian horizontal lines—and custom cabinetry. The dining room has a cozy feel despite the open floor plan, thanks to the large aquarium that anchors the space and provides a bit of seclusion from the entry foyer.

A mere eating counter divides the U-shape kitchen from the den, a setup that offers uninterrupted views of the den's fireplace, entertainment center, and the outdoors beyond via full-height glass patio doors.

To the right of the entry, an alcove hides a powder room and a stairway leading to the master retreat on the top level. That retreat features a wraparound deck, floor-to-ceiling doors, and operable windows, inviting the beautiful California outside to come in. On cooler days, the upstairs fireplace sparks cozy warmth. A room-size walk-in closet and a master bath with tub and shower that overlooks the

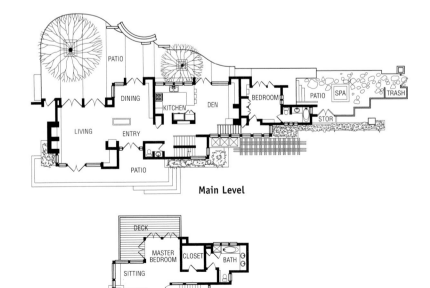

Main Level

Second Level

canyon complete the upstairs hide-away. A single door at the upper landing closes off the private retreat from the home's lower levels. (In fact, the house contains only five interior doors: one each for the three bathrooms, the guest room, and the master suite.)

Natural materials prevail throughout: granite floors, hearths, and countertops; maple kitchen and dining room cabinetry; Honduran mahogany architectural details and custom cabinetry; and 100 tons of rugged ledger stone used in the walls and fireplaces.

1 *The den combines the home's cardinal architectural materials with warmth and grace. A ledger-stone wall extends beyond the floor-to-ceiling windows, melding the indoors and out.*

2 *The master suite is a private hide-away that opens onto a wraparound deck accessible through wide single-pane French doors. The deck itself offers a secluded sitting area at treetop level.*

3 *An eating counter separates the custom kitchen from the adjoining den. The maple cabinets echo those in the dining room, and the polished granite countertop matches the stone floors used throughout the main level.*

Intriguing
International

1

2,900 sq.ft.

• This clean-lined style is marked by a neutral palette with bold bursts of color, unadorned geometric shapes, and industrial materials (large sheets of glass, steel beams, railings, and stanchions).

Views, light, and uncluttered space. That's part of the appeal of the International style, making it a particularly good choice for a location valued for its wonderful outdoor scenery. It's of a mind-set that wonders why anyone would distract from a breathtaking lake view with frilly window coverings and architectural ornament. Relentlessly practical, this house is crafted from low-maintenance industrial materials, such as glass, concrete, and steel, that allow its owners to spend more

time enjoying their location and less time performing building upkeep. The exterior is whitewashed cypress—harder and more rot-resistant than cedar and devoid of fussy frippery.

Inside, the living room is the home's focal point, with sweeping lake views through individual vertical windows grouped in a curve. As with the rest of the house, the overall palette is black, white, and gray, enlivened throughout with colorful artwork, flowers, and light-toned wood cabinetry.

The kitchen and dining areas are oriented to the east, where they get plenty of morning sunlight. The galley kitchen is wider than most, so there's room for multiple cooks. Within the work core are separate zones for food preparation and cooking. The refrigerator, wine rack, and

wineglasses are placed at one end of the room along with seating for non-cooks—a beverage and conversation area that serves well when entertaining guests.

Several pieces of furniture, such as the granite coffee table in the living room, the buffet and table in the dining room, and the media center in the family room, were custom-designed for the house and further emphasize its clean-lined style.

Another custom feature is practically a necessity: Each of the home's many windows is topped by a motorized blind. Not only do the window treatments maintain the sleek, uncluttered look essential to a home of this style, they make controlling the home's temperature possible, which is no small task given the large amount of glass in the design.

Style Notes

The Swiss-born architect Le Corbusier once described a house as a "machine for living in." The style he and 20th-century architects Mies van de Rohe, Walter Gropius, and Gerrit Rietveld founded and popularized became known as International style, named for the title of a 1932 exhibit at the Museum of Modern Art in New York. This crisp, modern style celebrates the no-nonsense aesthetic of the Machine Age and stresses functionality and flexibility above all else. Its design cues and favored materials borrow from industry: Unadorned steel, glass, and concrete predominate, as do simple geometric shapes (mostly rectangles, though a gentle curve appears here and there). Exteriors are often white stucco or wood siding and rarely brick and mortar. Huge unadorned windows often wrap around corners; interior walls are blank backdrops for art. Stripped of ornament and historical references, International homes are striking and dramatic, and in this postmodern, postindustrial age, they are beginning to acquire a nostalgic tinge as well. Call them the house of the future past.

2

3

1 *Standing like a monument on its manicured lawn, the lines of this International-style house are razor-edge clean. Nary a foundation planting or architectural ornament mar its dramatic monochromatic presence. What few details there are—the balcony railing and chimney, for example—are spare and industrially inspired.*

2 *An open floor plan, plentiful glass, and soaring 20-foot-high living room ceiling make the house seem larger than its 2,900 square feet. Stained concrete floors, chrome-and-leather furnishings, and a polished granite coffee table reinforce the industrial look, as does the catwalk's glass-brick floor above the staircase.*

3 *Clean is the style's watchword: A minimalist fireplace without hearth or interior chimney is topped by a thin flat dash of a mantle. Art alone adorns the walls; disappearing motorized blinds leave nothing between viewer and view. The Le Corbusier chaise longue in the lower right was designed in 1929 by one of the founders of the International style and complements the house perfectly.*

Main Level

Second Level

1 The opposite side of the efficient galley kitchen is a half-wall island that opens to the dining room.

2 Maple cabinets with plain fronts and full-length stainless pulls continue the linear theme. Everything else—even the black cookware on shelves beneath the cooktop—is black or white.

3 This built-in media center serves as both storage unit and focal point in the family room. The alternately spaced cabinets, shelves, and drawers act as a room divider and keep magazines, books, and other media tidy.

4 Located in a second floor loft space that opens to the living room below, this home office has spectacular lake views and a wide-open, unconfined feel that belies its modest square footage.

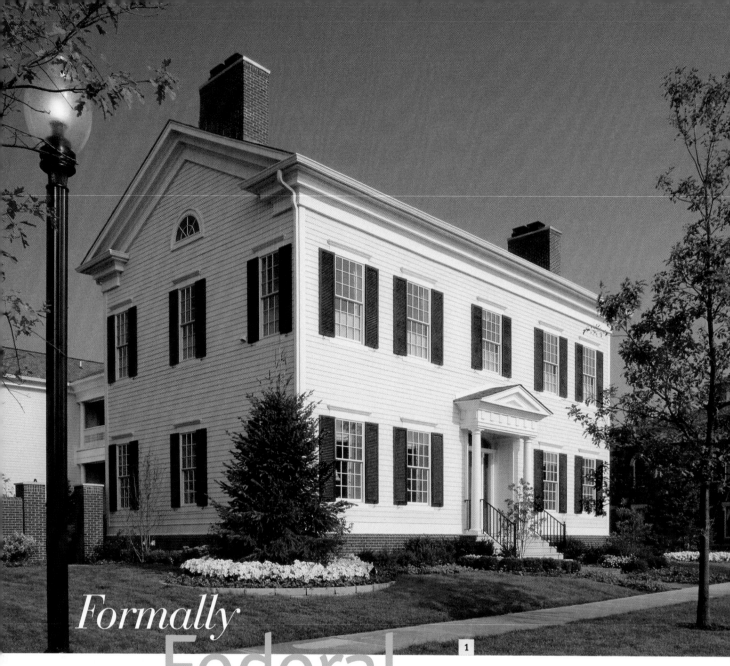

Formally Federal

3,500 sq.ft.

FEATURES

• From its classical proportions to its cornice moldings and brick foundation, this house exterior is pure Federal style. Though the interior makes use of the colors, hues, and patinas of time gone by, the floor plan is pure 21st century.

New homes can reflect classic architectural styles on the outside without sacrificing modern comforts on the inside.

From the street, this house appears to be from the Federal period or, at least, a very accurate reproduction. The look—formal, yet clean, simple, and unpretentious—has never fallen from favor. Yet the interiors of Federal homes, with small kitchens, narrow hallways, and compartmentalized floor plans, can be difficult to live in for any but the most dedicated historical purists.

This house combines the best of both worlds: a 19th-century enve-lope with a 21st-century floor plan. The front of the house starts off on a traditional note with a centered two-story entry that opens to a living room to the left and a dining room to the right. A library occupies the space behind the living room, but that's where the tradition ends. Behind the dining room, any semblance of a period floor plan vanishes as you walk into a large sunny kitchen with a big island. Beyond that, a breakfast area opens onto a

Style Notes

Popular from about 1780–1820, Federal style was an American interpretation of the English Adam style, which was inspired by classical architecture of Greece and Rome. Most Americans found the classical roots and proportions of the Adam exteriors appealing, but they considered Adam interiors too lavishly garish. American Federal style emerged as a somewhat simplified version of Adam architecture, featuring a balanced gable-end facade with a centered front door—often sheltered by a portico, topped with a fan-shape transom light, and flanked by sidelights. Heavy moldings, massive chimneys, and fan-shape or elliptical gable windows further characterize the style. Interiors substituted subdued colors for the bright hues popular in England and carved moldings for the gilt and marble details that proved popular overseas. In short, though the country had recently achieved political independence, its aesthetics were still dictated by the mother country of most of its residents.

1 This classic Federal facade with centered entry, fanlight transom, and balanced array of lintel-topped windows conceals a remarkably modern floor plan.

2 Muted colors, rich fabrics, and elaborately carved, white-painted moldings are authentic Federal-style details. Classical columns, garlands, and elliptical motifs were particularly popular in Federal homes.

3 A candelabra-style chandelier, wall sconces, and richly patterned and textured wallpaper further the period ambience in the dining room. Large windows admit plenty of natural light.

gathering room that overlooks a terrace. This contemporary wing continues to the laundry room, storage room, and three-car garage.

Still the home feels classic inside, thanks to thoughtful use of color, texture, and period-style moldings. Natural colors were popular during the Federal period, along with thick carpets and flocked wallpaper that displayed more than a hint of opulence. The creamy wallcoverings and rich carpets in this home's living, dining, and gathering rooms reflect this preference, forming an elegant yet understated backdrop for period-style furnishings.

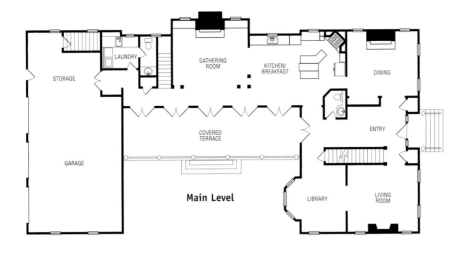

Main Level

STORAGE

LAUNDRY

GARAGE

GATHERING ROOM

KITCHEN/ BREAKFAST

DINING

COVERED TERRACE

ENTRY

LIBRARY

LIVING ROOM

Second Level

BEDROOM

BEDROOM

COMPUTER ALCOVE

BATH

BEDROOM

CLOSET

GALLERY

BATH

UPPER TERRACE

OPEN

UNFINISHED

SITTING

MASTER BEDROOM

3

1 An informal alternative to the dining room, the breakfast area keeps family meals in the kitchen. Muted greens and yellows used as accents throughout the kitchen further the home's color scheme while accenting the primarily white space.

2 A comfortable window seat makes an ideal perch for family members and guests who want to chat with the cook. Nearby, a pro-style range tucks into an angled niche to open up a wide traffic area.

3 Integrating a modern floor plan with a historical look is quite an accomplishment. This design maintains Federal-style exterior proportions for an authentic look from the street and fills contemporary needs for space by connecting the home to a garage at the rear. As a bonus, the inverted U-shape design creates a sheltered courtyard and an overlooking terrace.

4 A four-poster bed complements the home's high ceilings and vintage style. Understated colors and rich fabrics support the bed as the room's focal point.

5 A claw-foot tub, sconces, and built-in cabinets accent a long, narrow space reminiscent of dressing rooms in period homes. A mahogany vanity continues the period theme, its dark wood contrasting with the creamy colors of the room's decor.

4 5

Family
Farhouse

1

2,700 sq.ft.

2

F E A T U R E S

• A wraparound porch, asymmetrical design, one-over-one double-hung windows, and tasteful detailing characterize a house style that's an American icon.

If you're looking for a home that's as traditional on the inside as it is on the outside, you'll find this one especially appealing. The floor plan includes separate living and family rooms plus a semiformal dining room. This home is ideal for those who prefer cozy, well-defined rooms to large, open, multipurpose spaces. Benefits come with such a traditional approach: For example, having a family room adjacent to but separate from the formal living and dining rooms keeps messes and noise away

Style Notes

Formally called "American rural vernacular," this pleasingly simple, unpretentious style was popular in the decades surrounding the turn of the 20th century. A sort of simplified Victorian style, it retains the asymmetrical plan, dormers, gables, alcoves, tall windows, wraparound porches, and some of the detailing of ornate Victorian houses that preceded it. The house shown here, for example, features siding and trim in contrasting colors, exposed rafter tails, linteled windows, and just a hint of Gothic embellishment under the peak of one of the gables. Generally lap-sided with simple moldings and trim, and either metal or shingle roofs, these houses were less expensive to build and maintain than their gussied up, high-style Victorian counterparts. Popular in rural areas and small towns throughout the country, farmhouses such as this one are almost a Midwestern icon, as the style's ascendance coincided with the region's explosive population growth and house-building boom. The style remains attractive today: It's flexible, easy to build, adaptable to the use of contemporary materials (such as asphalt shingle roofing and synthetic siding), is light inside, and—thanks to those big windows and the neighborly porch—relates well to its surroundings. Most of all, farmhouse style homes have a familiar, homey, nostalgic feel with broad appeal.

from adult gatherings without requiring a frantic pickup routine before guests arrive.

This house also features a main-level master suite and extra space in the upstairs children's rooms. That means more room for young children and toys now and—even more importantly—plenty of space for teenagers and computer workstations as the children grow.

Most rooms in the house benefit from abundant natural light; it's one of the advantages to building on a big lot. On a larger piece of property,

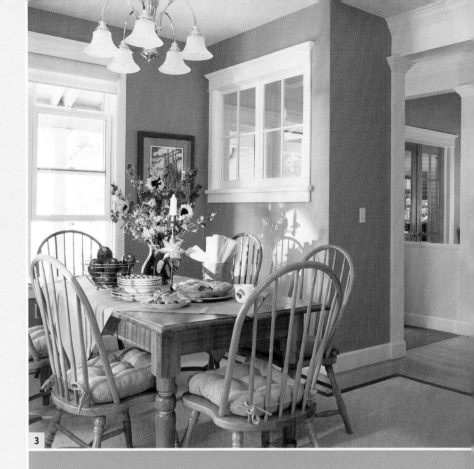

3

1 *Because of its simple, tasteful style, American farmhouses such as this one fit comfortably in almost any neighborhood. Country cousin to fancier Victorians, they harmonize well with other historic styles. Built on an infill lot in a suburban neighborhood or along with homes of more contemporary style in a new development, it invariably causes passersby to wonder whether it was the original farmhouse built before all the other houses.*

2 *At the hub of the house, the kitchen is perfectly located to support all eating spaces: the dining room, the breakfast nook, or the patio at the rear of the house.*

3 *The dining room, open to the living room and kitchen, benefits from multiple sources of natural light, including an interior window opening onto the entry foyer. Traditional casual furniture with familiar shapes and natural materials looks at home here.*

4 *In the farmhouse tradition, this home features a place inside the front door to take off footwear and hang jackets. A natural slate floor keeps damaging moisture away from the home's wood floors; mittens, boots, and hats are stored in the bench.*

4

you can design a house with rooms that jut out from the main mass, allowing light to easily flow from multiple directions.

The upper level is more open and relaxed than the home's first floor. Three bedrooms and an oversize bathroom all open onto a community play area. Instead of the long, dark hallway typical of older farmhouses, this modern version features an open playroom area with high ceilings. Interior windows also funnel some of the playroom's natural light into two of the bedrooms.

1 *The breakfast nook, located on the east side of the kitchen, makes the most of its sunny location with oversize cushioned furnishings and warm yellow walls.*

2 *A four-poster is the centerpiece of the master bedroom. High ceilings allow for a row of clerestory windows that admit natural light even when the main window blinds are lowered for privacy.*

3 *Dual pedestal sinks with custom mirrors simplify getting ready for the day. A nostalgic, black and white tile floor with black border and beaded-board wainscoting contribute to a vintage feel.*

4 *The living room borrows light and height from the switchback stairway. A mid-climb landing features a railed balcony that overlooks the living area.*

5 *Although comfortable on smaller lots, American farmhouses really shine when they're given room to breathe. A path, a patio, and plenty of room for flowerbeds and plantings give the porch and rear balcony a pleasant view.*

6 *The upper-level play area features French doors that open onto an outdoor balcony—and a loft level, accessible via a spiral staircase.*

Main Level

Second Level

29

Gently Georgian

4,000 sq.ft.

FEATURES

• This home's facade is a near-exact replica of the circa 1737 Red Lion Inn of Colonial Williamsburg, Virginia.
• The interior features a contemporary, open floor plan that combines comfortable modern living with a period feel.

This stately brick home with its 16 charming dormers, opposing chimneys, hipped roof, and intricate exterior brickwork is the new kid on its Greensboro, North Carolina, block. But its style is centuries older than those of its neighbors and proof that a house can be both an authentic-looking reproduction on the outside and full of 21st-century amenities and livability on the inside.

Built from one of 18 historical home plans in the Williamsburg Collection created by residential designer William E. Poole, the exterior of the house is accurate to within inches of the original.

Appendages in the rear of the house accommodate modern convenience. Here, the Red Lion stable becomes an attached garage, and the kitchen, bathroom, and laundry—separate outbuildings to the original inn—are absorbed into the home. With the addition of a 774-square-foot recreation room above the garage and a 240-square-foot screen porch in the rear, the original 3,200-square-foot inn grew larger by about 1,000 square feet.

On the inside, the details—elaborate moldings, heart-pine floors, multipaned windows, and high ceilings—are certainly colonial, but the floor plan is heavily updated. A kitchen opens to both a breakfast room and a great-room with a fireplace, built-in bookcases, and an entertainment center.

The three upstairs bedrooms have walk-in closets, and the master suite on the main level has screen-porch access, a walk-in wardrobe, and a bath with a whirlpool tub and double vanity.

1

Style Notes

As with the later Federal and Greek Revival styles, the appeal of Georgian-style houses—popular in this country from about 1715-1780—lies in the classical proportions, balance, and scale rooted in Greek and Roman design. The Venetian architect Palladio, one of the most influential architects of all time, popularized these design elements in England in the mid-1600s, and eventually they were imported to the new world via British house pattern books brought along by colonists. The home's height dictated the size of the windows, doors, and interior moldings, always maintaining classical proportions. In the South, Georgian homes often featured hipped roofs with chimneys on each gable end and dormers that lined up with the windows on the main level. For a pleasing look, dormer windows were smaller than main-level windows but used the same size panes. Brick was the most common building material, often laid in Flemish bond pattern, which alternated bricks showing end-out (headers) with bricks showing long-side out (stretchers).

1 *This new home draws its classical beauty from Colonial Williamsburg's 18th-century Red Lion Inn, named for the rampant red lion found on inn and tavern signage since the Middle Ages. A centered entry, steeply pitched hipped roof, symmetrical window placement, and massive brick chimneys characterize this authentically reproduced facade.*

2 *The mudroom connects the main house to a garage that's based on the original Red Lion Inn's stable. Stable-look doors flanked by carriage lanterns afford entry for two cars; an unfinished recreation room occupies the space on the second floor.*

3 *In keeping with the home's vintage spirit, some of the kitchen's natural-finish pine cabinetry have muntined pine doors. Honed granite countertop and white-painted crown molding add to the effect.*

4 *Rich tobacco brown walls and random-width plank floors unite the breakfast area with the great-room and kitchen. The large windows are reproductions of those in the original inn.*

Building a Reproduction

Building a house with authentic period detailing takes longer and costs more than building ordinary houses for several reasons. First, materials such as wood molding, heart-pine floors, and brick cost more than generic contemporary materials such as strip oak flooring and vinyl siding. Second, installing these materials in an authentic way, such as laying bricks in the Flemish bond pattern on this home's exterior, requires more highly skilled labor, more time, and greater supervision.

If you'd like to build a reproduction home from plans, you can get authentic-looking results only if you have a contractor who is accustomed to building such houses and a budget that allows you to follow the plans to the last detail. For best results, use a smaller crew and have the patience not to rush the project.

Some reproduction house plans, such as this one, offer colonial purists a resource list for finding authentic-looking details, such as dormer egress windows that resemble double-hung versions, properly scaled moldings, brick that looks handmade, reclaimed heart-pine flooring, and even functional shutter hardware.

1 *Just off the foyer, the formal dining room features heavy crown moldings, a chair rail, and a paint treatment that simulates wainscoting. The lower walls are cocoa brown and the upper walls are invigorating yellow.*

2 *To satisfy family-size storage needs, the back entry is outfitted with shelves and hooks for all kinds of gear. The stairway leads to an unfinished recreation room above the garage.*

3 *With architectural elements such as ceiling beams and a large-paneled fireplace, the great-room sets a classical stage that welcomes a range of furniture styles from colonial to casual contemporary.*

Main Level

Second Level

Enduring Craftsman

4,022 sq.ft.

• Traditional Arts and Crafts principles and details combine with modern amenities, such as vaulted ceilings and an attached three-car garage, in this contemporary interpretation of a classic style.

Craftsman bungalows have a romantic appeal that has never faded—their low silhouettes; broad, sheltering eaves; and wide porches hug the land in a romantic, English-cottage way. Inside, exposed woodwork, beams, and built-ins continue the appeal. Original period examples tend to be small, however,

1 *With its low, sweeping roofline, large porch, and extensive use of natural materials and colors, this home looks as though it sprouted from the soil.*

2 *A wall of windows floods the great-room with sunlight. Birch and cherry woodwork complement a mix of authentic Craftsman-style and modern furnishings. A vaulted ceiling adds volume.*

3 *The understated yet elegant kitchen lies at the center of the home. A raised soffit over the far counter houses light fixtures and defines the kitchen space without separating it from the adjacent great-room.*

Style Notes

"Have nothing in your houses that you do not know to be useful or believe to be beautiful," wrote William Morris, one of the founders of the Arts and Crafts Movement in England. The movement promoted the inherent beauty of simple, organic materials; natural colors; and fine craftsmanship. In the United States, those principles and ideals found expression in a short-lived but very popular architectural style that flourished from about 1905 until the mid-1920s. Characterized by low-pitched, gabled roofs with generous eaves, exposed rafter tails, and broad porches supported by tapered square columns, people often refer to these houses as bungalows. They're especially common in the West and are numerous in the Midwest and South. Interiors often feature an abundance of plain-sawn, naturally finished woodwork (usually oak), built-in furniture, bookcases, inglenook seating areas, tile fireplace surrounds, and flat-paneled cabinetry, (often with glazed doors). The style has enjoyed a renaissance lately because its natural materials appeal to an earth-friendly generation and its simple lines host vintage and contemporary furniture with equal ease.

and lack such contemporary amenities as attached garages, large kitchens, open gathering spaces, and adequate storage. Some people find the heavy oak woodwork a bit dark for modern tastes.

Fortunately there's a revival going on that lets you have your Craftsman bungalow and live comfortably too. This just-built example stretches the usually diminutive bungalow dimensions to more than 4,000 square feet. The trademark stone piers that support the porch

1 *Located just behind the kitchen, this breakfast nook feels wide open, thanks to transom-topped windows.*

2 *A bedroom bump-out creates space for a chest of drawers, allowing just enough room for a sitting area near the window.*

3 *Large corner windows and detailed woodwork brighten and warm the master bath.*

columns allow the plan to add a three-car garage to the facade without overpowering the home itself.

Inside, lighter birch and cherry woodwork in traditional Craftsman geometric motifs replaces darker fumed oak. Cross-beam ceilings—another traditional touch—are rendered in white paint rather than dark wood and appear decoratively on vaulted ceilings. Tall walls of windows bring in an abundance of natural light.

Finally, all those tasty period details adorn a contemporary floor plan that features an open, informal living area with a kitchen, breakfast room, and great-room.

The main level also makes room for a spacious master suite with its own bathroom and walk-in closet. There's also a combination laundry/mudroom located just off the garage. The lower level features three additional bedrooms with a centrally located bath, a wide-open recreation room, and abundant storage space.

Now that you've viewed a variety of architectural styles, this part of the book will help you get your project off the ground. By considering the specifics of your location and your home construction, you'll discover exactly what you want in your new home. Read the chapter in any order, but do read the whole chapter before you start building because the information overlaps and builds.

Your chief consideration. What features, neighborhood, commute, lifestyle, or price drive your choice of a new house and where it's located?

Your neighborhood. Will you choose a tract development, infill lot, or traditional neighborhood development?

Your lot. If you're a would-be country dweller who felt left out during the discussion of neighborhoods, pay close attention to this section.

Your siting options. Find out how to site your home on a lot to best take advantage of views, solar gain, and landscape options. Special sections address how to avoid buying a noisy lot and how to control and block noise.

Your building options. Find out what's entailed when you build a production house, a house from purchased plans, a systems-built house, and a custom house.

Your budget. Determine how much house you can afford and how to get the most for your money.

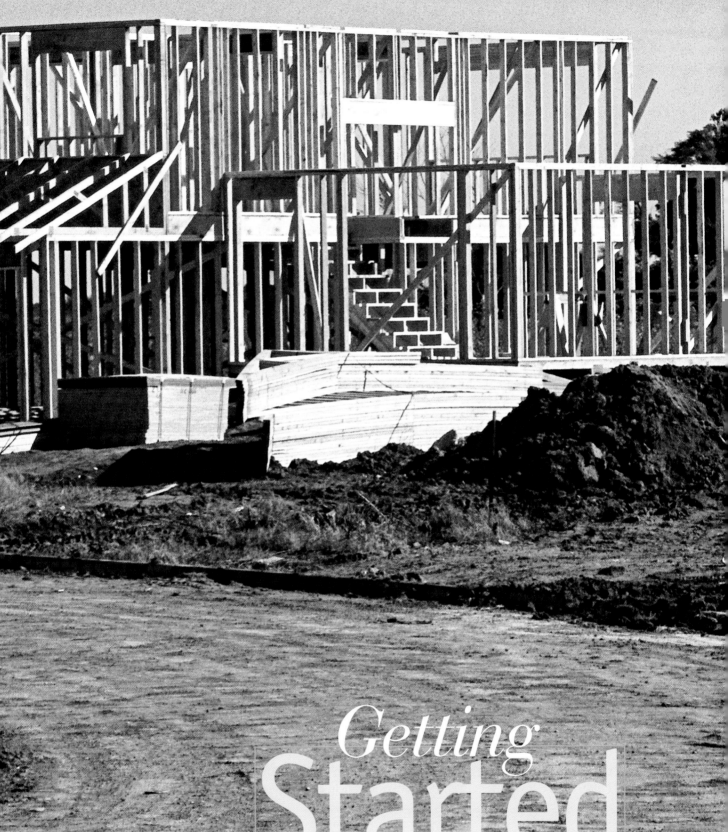

Getting
Started

1

The Right Location

Weigh many considerations when choosing a location to build, although one usually emerges as most important. Here are a few of the most common criteria and suggestions for how to consider all your options for meeting them.

Features: Even if you think you know what you want—a house in the country, for instance—it pays to trace back your thinking to what attracts you to that choice. Perhaps the draw of a country lot is a great view, access to green space, and the ability to be close to nature. If so, there are other locations you might consider. Many traditional neighborhood developments—those in which a cozy neighborhood of closely spaced new homes is surrounded by acres of green space, walking paths, and natural features—offer those amenities too. A suburban lot that abuts conservation land might offer everything you're looking for too. Before you decide on a particular area, think about what you specifically want from a location. Then ask yourself—and your builder or real estate agent—where you can find these features. The answers might surprise you.

Neighborhood: Perhaps your new home location is most important to you. You'd like to take advantage of a particular school district, for example, or live within the boundaries of a certain town, suburb, or neighborhood. If so, get a city map and outline the limits of the area you're interested in. When you see advertisements for lots or talk to builders about developments, you'll know right away whether the property you're considering meets your criteria.

Commute: You may want to limit your search to a maximum commuting distance from your work. If so, get out the map and a compass (the drawing tool, not the navigational instrument) and swing an arc around your workplace that represents the farthest you'd want to drive. (You might want to extend the distance somewhat along high-speed interstates.) Consider every neighborhood, development, and lot within that circle. If you're a two-career couple who works at different locations, swing two arcs: The areas where the circles overlap are your prime lot-hunting targets. If you plan to use public transport and are looking in a large metropolitan area, highlight the transport routes and stations on your map.

Lifestyle: If you would like to build a condominium in a recreation-oriented development, such as a golf, ski, marina, or beach community, you're looking for more than just living space—you're buying a lifestyle as well. Sales pitches for such places can be persuasive, so check out as many as you can before you narrow your search. Then put your toe in the water at your first choice for a year or more by renting a condo or staying at a resort there. Moor your boat in the marina, park your RV at a nearby roll-in resort, and think like a native for a while. If you'll be commuting to work, get a feeling for what the drive is like during rush hours in all weather and seasons. If you'll be commuting from your primary residence for weekends and holidays, test out the vacation traffic. What's the in-town traffic like? Are all the amenities you'll want available (not just luxury perks like poolside dining, but everyday necessities such as car repair, a good grocery store, and convenient medical care)? Subscribe to a local newspaper to get a sense for what the community is like and scan the real estate ads. A trial residence period also gives you a chance to look for local architects, builders, and real estate dealers and visit with knowledgeable locals about building options you might otherwise have overlooked.

Price: If your main goal is to get the most house for your money and you're working with a tight budget, look beyond sales prices and take the broadest possible view of housing costs before making your decision. Include all your housing-dependent monthly expenses—taxes, insurance, utilities, maintenance, commuting, education, and general cost of living. Sometimes the more expensive home turns out to be more economical in the long run when all these factors are considered. Two houses with comparable selling prices can offer living expenses hundreds of dollars apart per month.

Tract Developments

Think of new homes, especially in the suburbs, and you tend to think of builder developments like the one *opposite*—a landscape covered with new houses of the same relative size, each with its own plot of lawn. That's a widely available choice and often the simplest and least expensive option for buying a newly built home. Generally the builder offers several house plans to choose from, with many houses already under construction so the wait to move in is less. Not only the home but also the infrastructure itself—roads, sewer, water, and electrical service—is brand new.

Such neighborhoods can have their downsides too: lookalike houses, rudimentary landscaping, the dirt and noise associated with ongoing building, and the uncertainty of what the neighborhood will look like when surrounding woods and meadows give way to buildings. Also, if the scale of development is large and the pace rapid, the surrounding infrastructure—roads, schools, shopping facilities, public services—initially may be inadequate to service the influx of new residents.

Increasingly such neighborhoods are coming under fire for an additional reason: They contribute to sprawl. Such low-density neighborhoods in which each detached home has its own plot of green can devour land that might be better used for recreational, agricultural, or wildlife habitat purposes. Such neighborhoods can also increase traffic and commuting times and contribute to the decay of older suburbs and inner cities.

Tract development used to be the only choice for suburbanites set on buying new construction and is still an appropriate choice for some. However, you have other options. The following are two you might consider.

Infill Lots

If you want a new home but like the idea of living in an established neighborhood with mature trees, architectural variety, and a location closer to city amenities, consider looking for an infill lot—a vacant plot in a largely built-up area. Sometimes these are simply housing lots that have, for one reason or another, never been built on. Sometimes a homeowner with a double lot decides to sell half the holding, or formerly public land becomes available for private ownership.

Perhaps the land was once considered unbuildable because, for example, the soil wouldn't allow for septic tank percolation or was inappropriate for well drilling, or the cost of bringing in utilities was deemed too expensive. Or maybe the land was much steeper or more uneven, oddly shaped, or smaller than neighboring lots. Such drawbacks may no longer exist: Sewer lines and city water might have long since replaced septic systems and wells, for instance. Lots once considered undesirable or inconvenient to build on might have special qualities such as an interesting shape, a wonderful view, natural beauty, or a location that's become increasingly valuable. All are reasons that make these lots worth reconsidering.

If you find the right lot in the right area, you can have a new house and an older character-rich neighborhood too. Be prepared to do more work to achieve it, however. You'll have to put more effort into getting your house than simply walking into the nearest development showhouse, picking a model, and applying for a mortgage.

First you need to find a lot. Real estate agents can help, as can city governments, which sometimes have an inventory of property for sale. The best sources are often long-time local residents, who may know of neighbors with land that they want to part with. Another option is the drive-by buy: Look both for "for sale" signs and for unused property in neighborhoods that interest you.

Before you buy such a lot, consult with an architect and/or contractor—and perhaps with a civil engineer as well. An engineer and architect can be especially important if the lot poses some topographical challenges, such as steep slopes, ledges, drainage, or stability issues. Make sure the lot can support the kind of house you envision. With some care and creativity, you may find that a challenging lot has assets and character that a conventional plot of level lawn lacks.

1 *Lots on the fringes of tract development often look more attractive if they abut woods and meadows such as these. Unless the land is permanently set aside for green space, however, it may soon fill up with more houses.*

2 *Abundant pavement—in the form of broad streets, big turnarounds, and double-wide driveways—typifies tract development, as do houses of similar square footage, style, and lot size. Some like the clean, new, unified look; others find it sterile.*

Traditional Neighborhood Developments

Sometimes called "New Urban" or "Neotraditional" by architects and city planners, traditional neighborhood developments, or TNDs, revive many of the people-friendly features that made Main Street communities of the early 1900s so appealing: quiet streets, neighborly front porches, compact downtowns, and picturesque public spaces.

1 *Front porches and sidewalks dominate the streetscapes of traditional neighborhood developments, many of which feature backyard garages, narrow streets, and small front yards.*

2 *This TND in Wisconsin shows how mixed types of housing, commercial development, and green space can work together. This development features 40 acres of open space, including a 20-acre wetland park.*

Most TNDs are suburbs or separate towns near an established urban center, although they don't fit the mold of a typical suburb. They usually have a central business district, and homes sit close to the street on relatively small lots, with garages placed behind the houses on alleys. The streets are narrow and connect one neighborhood to another rather than terminate in isolated clusters or cul-de-sacs.

One reason for building closer together is to promote more neighborly contact. Another is to swap large, high-maintenance lawns in favor of smaller ones *and* more public open spaces that the whole community can enjoy.

To attract the mix of age groups and incomes that typified yesteryear towns, TNDs usually offer a range of housing types and prices, rather than one type and one price, typical of most tract developments.

Often options include apartments, townhomes, detached single-family homes, and live/work units—small business space at street level and living quarters "over the store."

To avoid visual clutter and pro-

mote social harmony, most neotraditional neighborhoods have a community-adopted design code. For instance, one Midwestern community specifies that all designs must be Arts and Crafts-inspired.

These communities are designed around people rather than cars and promote self-reliance. Small shops and village-center businesses are usually within walking distance of most residences, as are elementary, middle, and high schools.

Parks, green space, and wetlands are frequently incorporated in developments, and paths for walking, bicycling, and jogging often wind around the communities and their surrounding green areas.

Those designed as commuter communities often provide bus or rail service to the nearby urban center, reducing street traffic and commuting.

Some experts predict that TNDs will eventually replace tract development as land becomes scarce and more expensive, environmental concerns mount, and buyers are increasingly attracted to the quality-of-life benefits that such communities offer.

Still, these developments are not for everyone. First of all, although the concept is spreading, there may not yet be such a community underway where you want to live. Or you may need to live in one while it's in the process of development.

If you like a big yard, lots of privacy, and the freedom to build any kind of house you please, you might find such a community confining. You can generally buy a larger house on a larger lot in a tract development than you can in a TND, though many TND dwellers feel the benefits of living in a neotraditional setting and easy access to shared green space more than outweigh the cost differences.

Lot Choice

When it comes to the actual ground on which to build, you have many choices. Sifting through them and settling on a property requires diligent research.

Accessibility. Before you buy a lot, see what it's like to drive there year round (in all kinds of weather),

traffic, public transportation availability, and emergency facilities access. Find out what it will cost to build and maintain any private roads to your house.

Services and Utilities. If you're considering building in a rural area, police and fire protection might be miles, not blocks, away so ask

---

The Homesite Checklist
Consider these factors before deciding on a homesite. The answers will come from many sources: local residents, county or state government offices, newspapers, and your own experience in spending time where you would like to build. Other questions are best resolved by professionals, such as your real estate agent, a local lawyer, or geotechnical or civil engineer. Don't buy anything until you're satisfied with the answers to your inquiries in the following areas.

The Area
__ Climate (area and microclimates, annual snowfall or rainfall)
__ Commuting distances for work and errands
__ Pace of development within the region
__ Long-term road and infrastructure plans
__ Land price sales history
__ Prevailing breezes (for siting the house)
__ Drinking water quality and past contamination
__ Local building restrictions
__ Potentially disruptive activities: quarries, airfields, logging, livestock facilities

The Site
__ Flood plain status
__ Drinkable water sources
__ Water rights (where applicable)
__ Soil types and depths
__ Access roads and deeded easements
__ Site history and previous uses
__ Septic system suitability and permit process
__ Neighboring properties and their zoning
__ Property taxes and recent rate changes
__ Home siting options
__ Covenants and neighborhood charters

Services
__ School bus system and nearest school bus pickup point
__ Response times for fire protection
__ Availability of police protection
__ Nearest medical facilities and ambulance response times
__ Electrical utilities, rates, and connection charges
__ Telephone, television, and Internet services
__ Propane availability and costs
__ Postal service arrangements
__ Garbage disposal and recycling options

neighbors of property you're considering about response times. Even in suburbs, response times varies.

Country dwellers not part of a rural subdivision with a shared water source need a well along with pumping and filtering equipment. If your new house isn't on a lot already served by utilities, determine the costs of running services before you buy. Charges can range from modest to considerable to prohibitive. Check TV reception, and factor in upgrades, such as cable or satellite service, when budgeting for your property.

Development. After contacting local real estate agents, talk with local planning and zoning officials (look them up under "Planning" and "Zoning" in the local government pages of the local phone directories) and highway departments (look under "Transportation Department" or "Department of Transportation" in the state government section of the local phone directories) to ask about planned or proposed development in your area.

Consult with state or federal agencies that manage land near the land you want to build on. Their plans for using such property may affect your homesite. You don't want to find out after you buy that an airport, shopping mall, or highway is slated to come through.

Soil and water. Before you buy any rural lot, get a detailed soil and water analysis by a civil or geotechnical engineer. A thin layer of soil or bedrock can mean thousands—perhaps tens of thousands—of dollars in additional expenses to construct a driveway, foundation, or septic system, and easily compacted soils create long-term problems concerning the stability of your foundation.

Ask a local well-drilling contractor how deep you'll likely have to dig a well. For a shared well, ask what your maintenance and emergency repair responsibilities will be.

Legal issues. Consult a local lawyer for an opinion on what water rights will accompany your property and whether your deed will need to include an easement for crossing shared roads on other properties. If you're buying into a covenanted development or community, have a property attorney interpret the fine print for you before you sign a deed or contract.

Siting Options

Placing a house in the middle of a lot, with the front door facing the street, is the most common siting choice in many neighborhoods today. However, this is just one siting option, and it's often not the best. Your house may well be remodeled or relandscaped in the

future, but it probably will never be resited, so give thought to your choices. Optimal siting can make the difference between a noisy, uncomfortable, inefficient, awkward-looking home and a quiet, comfortable, energy-efficient, graceful one. Here are some siting issues to consider.

Inventory the lot's best features. Walk the land carefully at various times of the day and, if possible, in all seasons to get a sense of what you like best about it. Tie bright orange ribbons around trees and plants you want to preserve. If there are exceptional plants or small trees in what will become excavated ground or in the path of a roadway, consider marking them with different color ribbons for transplanting.

Note the best views and consider how you might place your house to take the best advantage of them. Consider prevailing winds—you may want to place aromatic shrubs or flowers so that pleasing scents waft across your screen porch or into your open windows.

Build on the worst part of your lot. All parts of a lot are not created equal. Perhaps a grove of trees has been mangled by a wind or ice storm or a corner of the land was scarred by a previous owner's misuse. Consider redeeming such places by siting your house there. That

way, you displace the damage, avoid disrupting your lot's best features, and avoid going to great trouble and expense to repair the damage.

Build to the north of the lot. In a Berkeley, California, neighborhood study, residents were shown a plan of their lot and asked to circle the areas in their yard in which they spent the most time. In nearly every case, they circled areas with a southern exposure. Like plants, people are drawn to sunlight. Make the most of your yard by building your house on its northern edge, leaving the sunny southern stretch for outdoor living.

Orient the floor plan to the sun. People have the same preference for sunny rooms that they do for sunny yards. If possible, stretch your house along an east-west axis and locate the most important rooms on the south side. Not only will these rooms enjoy maximum sunshine and a view of your south-facing yard, but you'll also enjoy lower utility bills because southern exposures get maximum solar gain in winter, minimum excess heat in summer.

Create outdoor rooms. When designing your house and any outbuildings, consider the shapes they make in the lot they stand on. People feel most comfortable when there's some feeling of containment.

They prefer courtyards, for example, to wide open spaces. To make the most of this preference for coziness, build a house that gives shape to the spaces that surround it. Then furnish and equip those spaces for the kinds of uses you enjoy most: gardening, relaxing, entertaining, sports, and family projects and activities.

To make these rooms even more attractive, plan to reduce noise and increase privacy by placing an outbuilding, such as a detached garage

or a sturdy fence, between your yard and a busy street, for example.

Plant strategically. Deciduous trees on the south side of a house provide cooling shade in summer and let the warm winter sun through after leaves fall.

Evergreens make windbreaks from northern blasts and absorb sound too. A tight evergreen hedge provides noise protection as far downwind as 20 times its height.

If space is a problem, vines on fences or low walls can be used as noise buffers, privacy screens, and shade. To increase protection, plant on berms (landscaped mounds of earth) or combine trees and shrubs between your house and a noise source.

How NOT to Site a House Much of this information may seem like common sense, and it is. But common sense and common practice are often in conflict. A thoughtless, destructive, bulldoze-and-build process is still fairly common. If you see these kinds of practices occurring in a development you're considering, you may want to continue your search. You—and the land you live on—deserve better treatment.

Removal of topsoil: If bulldozers are scraping the rich black topsoil off the subsoil of the development before houses are built, know that the developer is mining the rich soil and selling it—leaving the new homeowners with poor-quality subsoil that might make it difficult to grow grass, gardens, or even trees.

Removal of existing trees: Often contractors clear the land of all vegetation before building houses, then plant tiny trees after the houses are built. The process means houses can be built faster and equipment has easier access to the building site, but it denudes the land of its most valuable assets—mature shade trees.

Battering existing natural resources: Almost as bad as clear-cutting and bulldozing are contractors who leave mature trees standing but drive heavy equipment over their root systems, compacting the soil or scarring tree bark with passing. Such trees may look healthy for a season or two, but many eventually die of root compaction or trauma, leaving the new homeowner with the expensive problem of removal and replanting.

Make Lists!

You'll be happier with the house that you build if you know what you and your family need and want. Use the following checklist to develop a list. But don't stop there. Four bedrooms, two-and-a-half baths, and a three-car garage.... One plan that meets those criteria could be a dream home; daily life in another plan might not serve your dreams with nearly as much success.

As you review the houses in this book, think through a week, month, and even a year in the life of your family and new house. Think through what everyone will be doing and where. Do you need rooms arranged so that family members are in view but not on top of one another? Where will you be when the kids entertain friends? Too much openness can create a gymnasium atmosphere; too much separation can undermine shared experience. Think it through to achieve the bal-

Architectural Style It's not uncommon for today's homes to present one architectural style outside and another within its walls. Such a concept broadens your options considerably. Today's cozy Craftsman house can include vaulted, spacious interiors, and intimate rooms can be carved into a wide-open International floor plan. Working with an architect to mix themes assures quality and long-term appeal.

ance of togetherness and privacy that you desire.

Think too about feel and mood. When do you most enjoy the sunlight; when do you like to be in a large room or a more intimate, cozy one? The spacious environment of rooms with vaulted ceilings is well-known, but new trends cater to the yearning for cozy, comforting spaces. You can lower a ceiling or add beams

for greater intimacy in dining rooms or library corners. The point is, pay attention to what pleases you and seek it out. Otherwise, you may find yourself seeking refuge in unexpected nooks and corners.

Finally, don't feel as if you must include certain rooms. If a great-room supported by a family studio works better for your lifestyle than the traditional living, formal dining, and casual family room arrangement, go for it. It's worth spending extra time to find or create a home that suits you well, especially if you plan to live in the house for a long period of time.

1 *With a desk/work surface as part of this kitchen's island, one person can get dinner underway while the other completes work or home tasks—such as researching travel plans—within chatting range of each other. Handy cubbies keep things neatly organized.*

WISH LIST

Note each item that you need with an **N**; note each item that you want—meaning it would be nice to have but isn't essential—with a **W**. Use the Notes space that follows each section to describe in detail any specific features you'd like to include, such as roll-out drawers in kitchen cabinets or extra-tall bathroom counters.

PRIVATE SPACES

Bedrooms

___ Master bedroom
___ Master closets, standard
___ Master closets, walk-in dressing area
___ Master sitting area
___ Master mini-kitchen
   ___ mini-fridge
   ___ mini-counter
   ___ mini-storage
___ Additional bedrooms
___ Guest bedrooms
___ Additional closets

Notes

_____
_____
_____
_____

Baths

___ Master bath
   ___ standard shower
   ___ oversize shower w/bench
   ___ double shower
   ___ standard tub
   ___ jetted tub
   ___ soaking tub
   ___ single vanity
   ___ double vanity
   ___ standard toilet
   ___ enclosed toilet
   ___ enclosed bidet
___ Additional full baths
___ Additional half baths

Notes

_____
_____
_____
_____

PUBLIC SPACES

Family Spaces

___ Breakfast room
___ Formal dining room
___ Living room
   ___ fireplace
   ___ media niche
___ Family room
   ___ fireplace
   ___ television niche
___ Great-room
   ___ fireplace
   ___ media niche
___ Home theater
___ Family studio/Group computing/
Project room
___ Music room

Notes

_____
_____
_____

Personal Spaces

___ Home office
___ Library
___ Studio
___ Wine cellar
___ Music room

Notes

_____
_____

Kitchen, Primary

   ___ number of cooks
   ___ ovens
   ___ warming drawers
   ___ microwave oven
   ___ cooktop burners
   ___ range hood
   ___ sinks
   ___ refrigerators
   ___ wine refrigerator
   ___ refrigerated drawers
   ___ dishwashers
   ___ trash compactor
   ___ island
   ___ snack bar
   ___ countertop surface, in linear feet
   ___ cabinet storage, in linear feet
   ___ butler's pantry

___ walk-in pantry
___ pantry
___ recycling center

Kitchen, Supporting

   ___ small refrigerator
   ___ microwave oven
   ___ single oven
   ___ wine refrigerator
   ___ countertop
   ___ cabinet storage
   ___ snack counter

Notes

_____
_____
_____
_____
_____
_____

UTILITY SPACES

Garage

Note the number of cars you'd like to fit in the type of shelter.

___ Attached garage
___ Detached garage
___ Carport

Other

___ Front entry closet
___ Mudroom
___ Laundry
___ Workshop

Outdoor Spaces

___ Front porch
___ Back and side porches
___ Screen porches
___ Decks
___ Patios

Notes

_____

Siting Considerations

Early homesteaders lacked the equipment to build quickly, but they had an asset: time. They often camped on their homestead for a season or more, getting to know their land intimately, clearing it slowly, creating minimal site disturbance, and orienting the house with regard to sun, wind, and weather. The result was often a light-filled, energy-efficient house that made the most of its setting.

Take a look at the new house built in historic Norwell, Massachusetts, *right*. It looks like it has been there forever: surrounded by mature trees, welcoming sunlight, and prevailing breezes; gazing out at beautiful meadows and woodland vistas. The planning that went into achieving such harmony with nature holds lessons for any home builder.

Here's how to site and build your house with the same care:

Know your property. Walk your land in all seasons and all weather. Identify natural features you want to highlight or preserve. Note where the sun rises and sets in different seasons. Decide what views appeal to you the most. Obtain an enlargement of a geodetic survey (check with your state cartographer's office) that shows your lot. Study how the land slopes, noting what areas will best support a firm, dry foundation. Then, and only then, choose your building site.

Treat the land gently. If your site is wooded, thin brush and saplings by hand, gradually opening views without crushing delicate forest growth or scarring valuable mature trees with heavy machinery. For example, the historic Norwell home has its driveway routed around a beautiful pine, sparing a hemlock grove and a cluster of holly while adding graceful curves. The

1

drive's sinuous path also follows a subtle ridge line, reducing the amount of grading required, providing privacy, and keeping road noise from reaching the house.

Supervise the site work. Heavy equipment can damage a site, so lay out your expectations to contractors in advance. Use markers on trees and detailed verbal instructions to make sure bulldozers and excavators stay clear of trees, avoid compacting delicate root systems, and clear no more land than necessary. There's no sense in wiping the landscape clear of mature growth, then buying and planting small trees that won't look good for another 50 years. In the home shown *above*, the homeowner also instructed excavators to follow colonial prac-

1 *With a dry-laid stone wall, mature trees, native plantings, and classic design, this home fits right into its New England lot.*

2 *Many builders would have wiped out the clusters of oak and birch trees that shade this home's facade, leveled the site, and started from scratch. Care allows for the preservation of such priceless assets.*

3 *This plan locates the garage to the north, preserves mature trees that screen the east-facing facade, and makes the most of a sunny clearing to the south by locating flower beds, a dooryard herb garden, a grape arbor and patio, and the kitchen and family room along the home's southern side.*

tice and dig a shallow foundation hole—3 feet deep rather than the conventional 6 feet—and pile the fill around the edges to make up the difference. This results in less site disturbance, better drainage, and an authentic look. The process was also less expensive than hauling the fill away.

Orient the house carefully. Decide how various parts of your house will relate to the land before you design the structure. This home's kitchen is located on the south for maximum light and solar gain. Fragrant lilacs near windows catch southwest summer breezes, spreading their scent indoors and out. The garage is also placed to the north to serve as a bulwark against New England's thrashing winter storms.

Select your architect with care. Make sure the professional you choose is a good personality match, open to your ideas about historically informed siting, and knows or is willing to research the historical details you want to incorporate. (The owners of this home interviewed seven architects before finding the right match.)

Landscape with local assets. Native plants, which in this case include lilacs, mountain laurel, daylilies, and ferns, are easier to care for than generically selected landscaping species.

Seek local information. Local ecologically sensitive local architects and landscape designers can be your best sources of information on how to site a house. In addition, state and county extension offices may offer free or low-cost seminars and consultations on the subject.

Noise — It's invisible and sometimes easily overlooked when you're excited and focusing on such tangible things as lot characteristics and view. Subtly, over time, however, the static in the background can become the noise that annoys. Here's how to look for a lot that comes with peace and quiet.

Look at the topography. Houses built low and surrounded by hills or embankments tend to be noisiest because the surrounding barriers reflect and concentrate sound. In contrast, quiet houses sit up high, away from reflecting landforms. If you're building near a truck route, avoid a site that's within earshot of a steep grade. Trucks are loud when laboring up hills and can be even louder going down when they use engine brakes.

Consider the built environment. Large buildings can reflect unwanted sounds toward your site. The noisiest places are on traffic arteries set between tall buildings. However, large buildings can perform a service if they are between your house and the noise. If you're considering building on land near a major airport, check with airport officials about normal flight paths. The noisiest area is a three-mile-wide swath directly under these paths for 15 miles on either side of the airport.

Watch for trees and wind. Greenbelts or trees, particularly if they include mature evergreens and are at least 100 feet wide, can create pockets of quiet if located between your house and the noise. Check prevailing winds too: Ideally, you want to be upwind of the racket.

Test the site. If you're serious about a building site, visit it several times during the day. Sometimes an area that is quiet at midday is downright raucous at night or early in the morning. A site near a school, for example, is apt to be noisy before and after school and several times during the day.

Lend an ear to your neighbors. Auto buffs, music fans, and do-it-yourselfers might ply their noisy hobbies well into the night; partiers may be oblivious to their own racket.

Check for nearby construction projects. The building or improving of roads—or the construction or demolition of buildings—can rattle your china and your nerves.

Don't despair. If you find a lot that's noisier than you'd like, consider building a house of structural insulated panels or insulated concrete forms, which have dramatically lower interior noise levels. See "Alternative Building Materials," page 185.

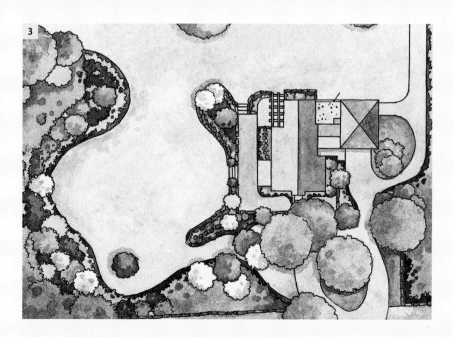

Design Strategies

Now you're ready to choose a house plan or help create one, if you're considering building a custom design. Whether you choose a production house or have one drawn from scratch, every new house is part choice, part creation, because you're bound to want to personalize your new home in some way, even if you're just choosing flooring, fixtures, and finishes.

First, though, you need to find a floor plan that suits your needs. Sifting through thousands of house plans—whether those offered by production builders, through systems-built house manufacturers, or in plan books—can be overwhelming if you haven't worked out a strategy. Start by thinking about what you want, need, and desire in a new home (see "Make Lists!" pages 46–47). Then examine what you like and dislike about your current home. As you look at each plan, ask yourself the following questions. (If you're going to be building a custom home, these same questions will help you prepare for your initial meeting with your architect or home designer.)

What does this home offer that you don't have now? Easy answers might include better storage, more bedrooms and bathrooms, or space for entertaining friends. Look beyond the obvious to see how the home will fit—and improve—your lifestyle.

Maybe the great-room will offer space for family activities that your current room can't accommodate, and the home office will mean fewer late evenings at work, freeing up more time for family fun. The main-level master suite and laundry room will decrease stair climbing. A larger garage might accommodate that boat you've always wanted.

What does your current home offer that you don't want to give up? You can easily take for granted your present home's best features and end up missing them terribly when you move to a home that lacks them. Make a list of your favorite things and make sure your new design includes as many of them as possible.

Will this home be big enough—or too big—in 5 or 10 years? Regardless of your current stage of life, a home that is just the right size now won't necessarily be just right in the future. A flexible house plan allows you to convert spaces as needs change.

A playroom can become a bedroom when another child is born. A child's bedroom can become a den or sewing room later. If a home office has an adjoining bath, it can be used as a suite for overnight guests, provide housing for an aging relative, or become your main-level master suite in later years.

Look for a plan in which seldom used rooms—or those that may be someday—can be grouped in a separate heating and cooling zone.

Does the home's design coor-

dinate with your proposed building site? Home designers recommend that you have a site before you select a plan. This allows you to compare the home with features of the lot and to envision how the home will sit. If the lot is narrow and deep, a wide, shallow home isn't the best choice. In some areas, zoning and regulations limit the height of a house or govern the minimum and maximum home size in terms of a percentage of the total lot size.

Where are the best views, and which rooms will get morning and evening sun? Having your lot before selecting a home plan lets you examine where sunlight strikes the site. Compare this information to the placement of windows in the plan to ensure the design takes advantage of the best views, blocks views that are undesirable, invites morning and evening sun where it is most needed, adds welcome solar gain in winter, and prevents unwanted heat gain in summer. You can usually move or resize windows as necessary, but take care to retain the appearance and structural integrity of the building.

Will this home fit in with surrounding houses? People generally choose to live in houses different from their neighbors. Make sure the design of the plan you choose fits the neighborhood, whether you build in a new neighborhood or on an infill lot in an older area with established homes. Subdivisions may have covenants that establish acceptable home styles for the area, so check regulations before you purchase a plan. In addition, consider the size of the home in relation to others in the area. A home that is out of scale with its neighbors looks out of place and may be harder to sell.

Will an existing plan require extensive changes to build the house you want, or might a custom design be better? Every home plan goes through some changes to meet local building codes, to match

2

the style of a particular neighborhood, or to suit individual needs and tastes. Changes such as modifying the facade or adding a garage stall are usually relatively easy, and most home plan companies and production builders can quote prices for making these changes. Before having extensive changes made to a plan, however, ask the designer, plan broker, home manufacturer, or builder about similar versions that might better match your needs. Companies sometimes offer several variations of their most popular plans. If you simply can't find a floor plan that you like or you want a house with an out-of-the-ordinary style, consider a custom design, and be prepared to pay more.

Are room sizes appropriate to how you'll use them? For example, a large master suite can take 20 percent of the space in a home, which is fine if you use the space for more than sleeping, such as to house workout equipment or a reading area. If you rarely spend time in the master suite, though, consider modifying the plan to convert some of that area to more functional space.

Are amenities more important than the size of the home? Generally speaking, your home-building dollars buy either space or amenities, such as stone hearths, built-ins, and architectural trim and details, which can give your home personality and allure. Decide which is more important. The temptation is to take your overall home-building budget and divide it by an average per-square-foot cost to yield the total square footage you can afford. Remember that an average cost gets you average amenities and finishes. If you want a higher level of either,

you have to enlarge your budget or decrease the size of your home. (For help estimating costs, see "Home Costs Per Square Foot" on page 59.)

Will the home's degree of openness work with your tastes in decorating? Eclectic decorating styles can work in almost any floor plan, but some styles are less forgiving. If your themes are consistent from room to room, an open floor plan will be fine. If varied furniture styles or a preference for using many colors is your style, a more traditional floor plan with separate rooms might be a better choice. At the very least, consider how your furniture and decorating preferences can blend into the plan you are evaluating.

Are there spaces for special-interest rooms, such as hobby areas or exercise rooms? As you figure out the types and sizes of spaces within your home, remember the fun stuff. If you like to read, include a book nook. Add a third garage bay to house a workshop or potting area. A recent trend in home design is to include a family activity center where family members can pursue their hobbies. If budgets are tight, consider having specialty spaces built but left unfinished for now. Doing so is more economical than adding on later and can also be attractive to a future buyer.

Your Production Home

One of the quickest and often one of the least expensive options when purchasing a new home is to buy a home built by a production builder in a tract development. If you choose a home that's already built or close to finished, you get the additional advantage of an even earlier move-in date and the ability to see what the finished house looks like before you buy.

If you have more time and can involve yourself earlier in the building process, you can usually tweak a plan somewhat to make it fit your taste and lifestyle, although you don't get quite the selection you get by working with a smaller semicustom builder or with an architect.

Your chance to make modifications generally comes before construction starts, at what's often called a "plans-and-specs" meeting with the builder (if you're working with a real estate agent, bring him or her along to inform you of how any changes you're thinking of making might affect the home's resale value).

At the meeting, you get to select the floor plan (from a number of stock options) and basic finishes for the house. These may include:

- Floor plan changes
- Exterior siding and brick
- Entry door color
- Cabinetry and countertop colors
- Flooring
- Finishes (ceiling, wall, and trim colors)
- Hardware (cabinet pulls to entry locksets)
- Extras, such ceiling fans, cable

connections, and built-in light fixtures.

In some cases, you might be able to spec changes such as eliminating a dining room in favor of a larger kitchen, adding wood floors in place of wall-to-wall carpeting in the entry or kitchen, or adding light fixtures, ceiling fans, or built-in speakers. You also might add another stall to the garage—or, if the lot isn't large enough, extra width to accommodate storage shelves. If the house has a basement, you may also be able to spec anything from the complete finishing of that level to installing such things as a walkout entrance and roughed-in plumbing, both of which prep the space for later completion.

Many production builders charge an additional change fee for any changes requested after a certain date—even if the change is a deletion—so it pays to think through the plan carefully up front.

Some production builders offer a home network system—the installation of wiring for audio, video, telephone, or computers—as part of a basic package or as an upgrade. Others do not, so find out early on what your options are and whether you need to find a specialty contractor for this service and coordinate that contractor's work with that of the builder.

Generally there's a pre-drywall inspection of the house after the structure is up and before the interior walls are enclosed and finished. At this inspection, a builder's representative and the homeowner walk through the house, checking to make sure that the house matches the marked-up version of the blueprints that were generated at the plans-and-specs meeting. To make sure everything checks out, a final walk-through should happen before the builder hands you the keys.

Your Plan-Built Home

Another new construction option is to buy a set of plans and have them built. A middle ground between a full custom house and a production model, this choice can offer the best of both worlds: You get much greater selection without the additional costs of hiring an architect and without the additional effort of working through the home design process with him or her.

On the other hand, building from plans can offer the worst of both worlds, especially if you want to make changes to the plans. The process is nearly equal in complexity to the process of building a custom house, without the advantages of having a home that's designed just for you.

Advantages
- You can leisurely browse thousands of home plans in publications.
- Catalogs are inexpensive.
- Stock plans are created by architects and designers specializing in residential design.
- You save time and architect fees.
- Plans are prepared for builders to make bids, making it easy for you to determine what the house will actually cost to build in your area.
- You can make plan changes.
- You control the selection of construction and finish materials.
- If the plan has been built, you might be able to look at interior photographs or visit the home before you buy.
- Plan services research their designs for mass appeal and resale value.
- New plans incorporate current design trends.

Disadvantages
- If you require more than superficial changes to a plan, final costs may rival drawing a custom plan.

- Buying a plan based on an artist's rendering sometimes results in surprises: A house that looks good in an exterior illustration could have interior design flaws that are difficult for a layperson to spot in a plan. These defects can be expensive, or impossible, to correct after the house is underway.
- Many production builders won't build from plans other than those that they offer, forcing you to get bids from smaller, custom, or semi-custom builders, who typically charge more.
- Unlike production house arrangements, you are responsible for finding a lot and choosing all materials and finishes, rather than simply selecting from a limited list of options. This adds to the complexity of the project for you.

It's a good idea to have an architect review any plans you want to buy—and to personally visit the plan-built home you're considering and talk to the owners about the building and ownership process. That way, you'll know exactly what you're getting before you start.

If you can find a home that suits you perfectly as designed, building a plan house can be a good bet. Beware, though, of falling in love with an illustration or building a house that will require lots of tweaks to make you happy.

Your Systems-Built Home

The term systems-built homes refers not so much to a type of home as it does the building method. For example, log homes have a distinctive look; but for the most part, systems-built describes the materials used and the way those materials are assembled.

The three most popular types of systems-built homes are log, modular, or panelized components that are produced in a factory, then shipped to and assembled on your building site and foundation. They adhere to the same state and local building codes as site-built housing,

1 *Review plans carefully and ask your builder what alterations are possible. as A follow-up, make sure your changes are noted on the plans and that you get a revised set of plans that reflect the changes.*

1

and in some cases, quality is even better because of precision jig-built components and a climate-controlled factory environment. Systems-built house manufacturers offer a wide variety of architectural styles and floor plans. Many manufacturers will customize floor plans the same way a production builder might or even build a custom house from architect-drawn blueprints.

Although they are called systems-built, they also may be referred to as "prefabricated" or "factory built," but never "manufactured." The latter term, synonymous with "mobile," refers to houses that are built to a less stringent code standard. A chief advantage of systems-built houses is that they go up fast. On average it takes four to eight weeks' time to complete a systems-built house.

Because factory-built homes are built in highly mechanized factories under controlled conditions, final costs can be less than those for site-built homes. They're an especially good choice when local labor is in short supply, when you have a short building period or a looming deadline, when you're building on an infill lot and want to minimize dis-turbance to the neighborhood, or when you want a home with a distinctive look or specific energy-saving advantages that traditional stick-built homes don't offer.

Many different types of house styles and construction methods are available from systems-built home manufacturers. According to the National Association of Home Builders Building Systems Council, log, modular, and panelized homes are most common.

Log home companies produce factory-made or handcrafted log homes with solid log walls ranging from 6 to 15 inches in thickness. A wide variety of wood species, log profiles, joint details, and stock floor plans are available. Many log-home companies will modify stock plans or produce custom designs as well. For an example of a custom log home, see "Contemporary Cabin" on page 126.

Modular homes are 90 to 95 percent complete when they are shipped from the factory to the building site, where they are affixed to a conventional foundation. Two or more sections, 12 to 16 feet wide and up to 60 feet long, are delivered by truck and erected by crane to create the finished building. Modules also can be stacked to make two- or three-story homes. For an example of a modular home, see "Factory-Built & Fabulous" on page 94.

Panelized homes are constructed on site from factory-built wall panels. Panelized homes built with conventional stud walls are constructed of one of two types of panels: Open panels contain exterior sheathing only; plumbing, wiring, insulation, and sheathing are installed at the building site. Closed panels are finished interior walls that contain insulation and electrical and plumbing systems.

1 *This modular home was trucked to its prepared site, then a crane lowered it into place.*

2 *Modules can be joined and stacked to create houses of just about any size, shape, or design. This story-and-a-half Cape Cod cottage is one example.*

3 *Walk through the house with your builder's representative prior to drywall installation to make sure that any changes you requested on your blueprints have been properly executed.*

1

2

Panelized homes are constructed either of conventional stud-wall construction or super-strong, superinsulated Structural Insulated Panels (SIPs), which are panels of rigid foam insulation sandwiched between two sheets of structural plywood or other engineered wood product such as Oriented Strand Board (OSB). For an example of a panelized home, see "Scandinavian Country Cottage" on page 86.

For more information on systems-built homes, contact the Building Systems Council of the National Association of Home Builders at www.nahb.org.

Your Custom-Built Home

Building a custom home—as opposed to a home with a few custom features—requires a step up from the preceding options in complexity, time, and expense. The result can be a home that fits you and your lifestyle, takes advantage of the site perfectly, and has a higher resale value. In the same way you won't recognize the comfort of a custom-made suit until you have one, you might not be able to appreciate the pleasure of a custom house if you haven't lived in one. Few who have experienced custom homes would ever choose otherwise.

Building a custom house means starting from scratch. You select the home's lot and an architect or designer, who then helps you select a builder. Then you work with your team (which may also include a landscape designer, kitchen/bath designer, and interior designer) to compose your new home.

Choosing Pros

Choosing the best professionals to design and build your home makes your entire experience more enjoyable and ensures top-notch results.

Whether you're searching for an architect, an interior designer, a kitchen designer, or a builder, use

3

these tactics to connect with the best one for you.

Gather. Collect names of professionals to investigate and interview. Ask friends and colleagues for suggestions and recommendations. Identify local referrals with the help of professional organizations such as:

• American Institute of Architects (AIA) (800/242-3837, www.aiaaccess.com)

• American Institute of Building Designers (AIBD) (800/366-2423, www.aibd.org)

• National Association of Home Builders (NAHB) (800/368-5242, www.nahb.com).

Explore. Call the architects and contractors on your list—at least four to six from each profession—and ask for references. Then contact the people they name and ask them to recount their positive and negative experiences. If you see a recently built house that you like, contact the homeowners and ask for the names of the professionals they worked with and their experience and results.

Evaluate. Based on these references, interview the top three professionals who make the cut and tour some of their finished projects. Savvy architects, home designers, and builders will ask you questions as well to determine your expectations and needs. The goal is to come away from each interview and tour with an idea of the quality of their work and how well your personalities and visions match.

Solicit drawings. To narrow your choices to two or more architects, it might be worth the additional cost to solicit preliminary drawings from each one. This is a way to test your working relationship. In the same vein, ask builders for bids. Don't base your decision on cost alone. Instead weigh what you learn in the interview with the thoroughness of the bid. Your relationship may ultimately be more important than a small difference in job price.

The Professionals – What They Do

ARCHITECTS. An architect's schooling and training includes a five-year degree and a three-year apprenticeship in building design. Some have diverse practices that includes commercial and industrial buildings; others specialize exclusively in home design. An architect may charge by the hour, by a percentage of construction costs, by the square footage or number of rooms, by using a flat fee, or by any combination of these. Generally, an architect's services will cost approximately 10 to 15 percent of the total construction costs, although this varies considerably depending on the services rendered. The cost is often at least partially offset by the architect's ability to save clients' money through the use of ingenious design or creative material choices. (Home designers' training and experience vary widely; their services are generally less costly.)

According to the American Institute of Architects, a good architect will:

Analyze your wants and needs by asking you a wide range of questions about your housing goals and outlining the scope of your project.

Marry your goals with practicality by helping you make decisions concerning how your new home will function, what it will cost, and what it might be worth in the future.

Design for your future by providing a design that's flexible enough to accommodate your changing family size or reduced mobility as you grow older, helping choose amenities that can affect long-term value and resale, and proposing ways to lower energy and maintenance costs.

Visualize the design using rough sketches or computer-generated renderings. The architect might also provide three-dimensional renderings, build models, or stake the actual site so you can see how traffic flow, access, and views will work in your new home. Some architects provide interior design and landscape design services as well.

Act as your advocate during the building process by making sure your home is built as designed, and by helping the contractor resolve any unexpected difficulties that occur during the construction process.

INTERIOR DESIGNERS. Building a home, custom or otherwise, requires that you make an almost overwhelming number of choices about trim details, paint, flooring, hardware, and lighting. Many people become overwhelmed and make simple, neutral choices with the idea of personalizing the home later. You can shortcut that redundancy—and significant expense—by hiring an interior designer as part of your new home-building team. Interior designers can:

Simplify the selection of trim, cabinets, counters, flooring, paint, hardware, lighting—the list of things to decide upon goes on and on. Your designer can whittle an array of choices to a few, saving you time.

Incorporate your ideas and suggest others to enhance them.

Help you envision the look by using colored drawings and design software.

Give you courage. Simply seeing their work in other homes, or in your own, can give you the confidence to try a bold color or design.

Introduce products and techniques that homeowners don't normally come by. Designers know what's available and what services various manufacturers provide. They often discover intriguing options at the same price as stock goods.

Execute a look with unique details and color palette that creates smooth transitions and heightened impact.

Ensure that there's a place for the things you already own. You probably have a collection of furniture and other treasures you'd like to showcase.

BUILDERS. A contractor who specializes in building custom homes runs a very different business from a large production builder. A custom builder might build as few as one or two houses a year, compared to the production builders' dozens or hundreds. Builders are responsible for turning your architect's plans into your finished home. A good custom builder will:

Serve as part of the initial team, providing a craftsman's insight to the execution of your design in the most professional, cost-efficient manner possible.

Select the best subcontractors from among those available in your area to execute your particular home's design.

Schedule the work to ensure that the job flows sequentially, that materials are available as they are needed, and that coordination between the various trades on the job runs smoothly.

Supervise the job to make sure the blueprints are interpreted correctly and workmanship is high quality.

Communicate with the architect and homeowner, keeping them informed how the project is proceeding and involving them in decisions that need to be made as work progresses.

Your Role, Your Budget

Your part in building a custom house is a considerable one. As a client, you're not only the check writer and the home's ultimate inhabitant but its "parent" as well. Your needs, wants, and desires are its reason for being, and your taste and decisions shape its development. Yours is not a role to be taken lightly, for much will be asked of you along the way. And, like having a child, building a new custom home can test your discipline, patience, communication skills, and your marriage—not to mention your financial resources. Here are some tips to help the new home-building process go as smoothly as possible.

Do your homework. Before you commission a custom home, review home plan books and home manufacturers' catalogs, and take a look at new homes at open houses in your area.

Preliminary research is important for two reasons: to make sure that what you want isn't available "off the shelf" and to sharpen your own sense of what you like and don't like with regard to architectural style, amenities, features, floor plans, lots, neighborhoods, and sites. What you learn will be invaluable when working with your home's designer and builder.

Be thoughtful and open to ideas. When building a home, it doesn't pay be an autocratic know-it-all who demands that everything be done exactly according to your every whim. Such an attitude rules out the better results that the collaboration of a dedicated team can bring. It also usually increases costs and wins you the Client-from-the-Underworld award from your builder, architect, or interior designer. As a result, your team will

be much less likely to go the extra mile for you—something that a good relationship is much more likely to inspire.

Be decisive when necessary. Building a custom home is not a project for wimps. You can't delegate all the decisions that will comprise your satisfaction to other professionals, no matter how talented or competent they may be. You'll be called upon to make thousands of choices throughout the design and construction process. If you're intimidated by that prospect or find making up your mind difficult, consider an already designed or built new home.

Know the limits. Understand the bounds of your own expertise, talent, and budget. Be up front about these and ask your team to help you find ways around them. If you're not particularly adept at color or design, for instance, seek guidance in those areas. If you're technically naive about building processes or materials, ask for explanations as you go along. If visualization is a problem for you, ask for a drawing or rendering. If you'll be unavailable during a certain period of the building process, inform your team so the schedule can be arranged to accommodate your absence.

Communicate clearly. The house that gets built is the house that gets communicated, detail by detail, to the designer and builder. So be as clear, concise, direct, and articulate as possible when discussing your project with your team.

Make notes of points you want to make before meetings and refer to them during your discussions. Take notes of decisions you need to get back to your team about.

When you're talking, pay attention to the times when your language becomes vague or non-committal—that generally means you're not clear in your own mind about what you want. Tell your team you'll think about the issue and get back to them rather than leave them with ambiguous feedback.

Also, if you're part of a couple, designate one of you as the go-to decision person for questions from the team. That person takes down information, talks to his or her spouse, and gets back to the team. Such an arrangement prevents a builder, for example, from getting conflicting responses from each homeowner. It also prevents confusion between you and your spouse about who is supposed to talk to whom about what.

Be flexible and realistic. The rest of your team and those they hire to build your house are fallible human beings. Like you, they'll make mistakes. Weather, materials, supplier problems, permits, and a host of other details can—and probably will—conspire to delay your project, increase its cost, or cause it to evolve in unforeseen ways over the course of its completion. An ability to take the unexpected in stride and respond with good humor and a problem-solving attitude will go a long way toward making your project as successful and enjoyable as possible.

Your Budget

Determining how much house you can afford isn't as simple as going to the bank and seeing how large a mortgage you qualify for. Here's how to come up with a better assessment—and how to determine how large a house you can afford.

Consider All the Costs

Before you commit to a specific location, neighborhood, lot, or house plan, run some numbers yourself. A thorough estimate includes monthly commuting and other transportation costs, utilities, insurance, and maintenance expenses. For purposes of example, you're a two-career couple with a double commute driving two SUVs to different locations from a remote rural site. You live in a large country house heated by trucked-in (and therefore expensive) liquid propane gas, and you pay to have a long private lane cleared of snow in the winter.

In such a scenario, you might find that your monthly expenses alone—before you even look at a mortgage payment—have soared hundreds of dollars a month or more over your previous costs of living in a close-in suburb, and that these expenses put a good size dent in what you can afford to pay for a lot and home.

On the other hand, if you're moving from that same suburb into a TND with public transportation to work and a compact, energy-efficient home, you might actually reduce your living expenses compared to your current costs, allowing you to afford a larger mortgage than you expected. See "What Will Your New Location Cost?" worksheet, *below*.

Cost-of-Living Differentials

If you're moving to a different city or area of the country, consider the difference in regional costs of living as well. Fortunately you can use a variety of online calculators that make this task easy. Check the following websites for more information:

- www.bankratemonitor.com
- www.virtualrelocation.com
- www.relocationcentral.com
- www.homefair.com
- verticals.yahoo.com/cities
- www.runzheimer.com

On bankratemonitor.com, for instance, you can choose the city you presently live in, choose the city you're moving to, enter your current income, hit the Calculate button, and the calculator figures the percentage difference between the two cities and the income you'll need in the city you're moving to in order to maintain your current standard of living. If your income will remain the same, multiply your projected monthly budget by the percentage difference to get an accurate sense of what your actual expenses will be.

Mortgage Payments

After you estimate your non-mortgage expenses, you can calculate how much mortgage you can afford. The website www.bankratemonitor.com features a How Much House

---

What Will Your New Location Cost?

Here are some items to consider when comparing expenses. Add or delete categories to suit your family's lifestyle.

	Current Location	New Location
Income		
+Salaries		
His		
Hers		
+Investments		
+Other		
=Total Income		
Expenses		
+Housing		
Monthly mortgage		
Condo fees		
Homeowner's insurance		
Maintenance		
Other		
Utilities (water, gas, electric, cable, phone)		
Trash collection		
+Taxes		
Real estate taxes		
State and local income taxes		
Sales taxes		
+Transportation		
Commuting costs, parking		
Vehicle monthly payments		
Gasoline		
Auto insurance		
Auto maintenance		
Auto registration fees		
=Net Expenses		
Total Income		
-Net Expenses		
=Bottom line		

Can You Afford? calculator. It asks you to input your gross monthly income, new home down payment, loan term, interest rate, and other expenses; then it comes up with both an affordable mortgage payment and an affordable home price. Click on the site's Mortgage Calculator feature to experiment with different combinations of down payments, terms, and rates to see the effects of these variables on your monthly payment.

Home Costs Per Square Foot

Now the big question—how much house does that mortgage payment buy you? In other words, how large a house, in square feet, can you afford?

The answer depends on a host of variables, including your location, the house design and materials, the level of detailing, and the quality of the home's components from appliances to fixtures to finishes. Of course, you're wise to talk with several builders who work where you'll build and at the level of detail that you desire.

Fortunately, there's a comprehensive source that allows you to quickly estimate costs for the home you'd like to build.

The source is *Means Square Foot Costs*, a comprehensive reference guide published annually by R.S. Means. The book is the standard reference for building professionals, who use it to estimate job costs and calculate bids. If you're working with an architect, see whether he or she has a copy you can borrow. If not, it's well worth buying your own. (See www.rsmeans.com for more details.)

Means Square Foot Costs can give you an estimate of what your house costs to build in your location on several different levels. The book has square-foot cost estimates for 100 standard structures, including

---

Don't Forget the Furniture | It's easy to get so caught up in planning a new home that you overlook such comfort issues as furnishings, heating, cooling, house-cleaning, and yard care. Take a look at these costs before you finish your plans, so you'll be happy—rather than overwhelmed—in your new home.

Furniture. What furnishings will you use? Existing or new pieces? If you're moving to a bigger house or one with more rooms, browse a catalog or two to estimate what you'll spend furnishing it. Depending on your tastes, you can easily spend a few thousand per room.

Window Coverings. The costs for draperies and blinds add up quickly, yet they're essential for privacy and light control. If you don't want to plan your treatments exactly, contact several window covering companies and get estimate figures for the cost of blinds per square foot to help you plan for this cost. Research discount blinds providers—many offer top-of-the-line goods, but they still cost a substantial sum.

Heating and Cooling. Find out utility expenses for homes with similar square footages, rooms, and layouts, or show your home plan to a qualified heating, ventilation, and air-conditioning contractor for an estimate of costs. Moving from a three-story home to a ranch style of the same square footage can add more to your monthly bills than you may think.

House Cleaning, Lawn Maintenance, and Snow Removal Services. Ask the providers that you use now to give you an estimate for what the same services at your new home will cost. If you'll be using new providers, ask your new neighbors for recommendations and request bids from those providers.

Social Costs. What's the lifestyle like in your new neighborhood? Spend some time there to get a feel for it. It can cost you, not only in terms of money, but in spirit. Do the neighbors mingle? Do kids play outside? What interests do people have? If all the neighborhood kids attend private schools and get new cars when they turn 16, you need to know ahead of time that this is the sort of environment you and your family will be living in.

---

single-family homes of various sizes, and it also includes costs for typical modifications, add-ons, building components, and location factors arranged by zip code.

With this source in hand, you can quickly get a sense of how large a house you can afford or how much a house of the square footage you're considering building costs. As you develop your plans, you can use the book to fine-tune costs as you go and quickly trade off, for example, what the cost of an additional bathroom would be compared to a 10×12-foot deck.

The book also provides a benchmark figure against which you can compare bids from various contractors (if you're building a custom

home), or a way to evaluate whether upgrades in a semicustom or production house are priced reasonably. The book even includes a glossary of unfamiliar terms, so you can better understand the jargon your pros use.

What you'll find, not surprisingly, is that all houses trade off square feet for features and amenities. You can either have a larger house with fewer amenities and detailing and more base-quality components, or you can have a smaller house with more features and detailing and high-quality components. Chapter 4 more specifically addresses how to find the optimum balance—and how to get the most house for your money.

New house case studies

pack this section: photos and floor plans of freshly built houses to inspire your own ideas and choices. Slipped in among the case studies you'll find idea files, pages that focusing on a specific homebuilding topic, such as ceiling treatments, foyer design, and attractive garage strategies. You'll see the work of architects, residential designers, builders, interior designers, and homeowners. Most of these homes are not pure renditions of an architectural style, but are drawn from them, showing how various style inspirations can be attractively shaped to meet the needs and tastes of those who will live in them.

The case studies are arranged in three square footage ranges: Up to 2,500 square feet; 2,500 to 4,000 square feet; and more than 4,000 square feet. Certainly one size range will make sense depending where you're building, your needs, and budget. Browse them all, however, imagining your family, friends, and lifestyle in the spaces. Make notes of things you like—a floor plan or trim detail or storage solution—and those things you don't care for. Whether you choose a production home or work with an architect to create a custom design, knowing your likes and dislikes puts you in a better position to choose a home design that you love to come home to.

Case Studies

Tranquil Timber-Frame

1,300 sq.ft.

Douglas-fir timbers with hand-mortised joints make this Colorado cabin look right at home in the woods.

Although it's only 1,300 square feet, this tiny abode delivers big satisfaction. Built by a professional timber framer as his own retreat, the home looks and lives large because of its vaulted ceiling, robust beams, light-filled loft, wraparound porch, and upper-level deck. The house features plenty of windows and is sited on the edge of a small clearing in the woods, garnering maximum exposure to sunlight.

The timbers were built in a remote workshop then transported to the site where the traditional mortise-and-tenon joints were cut with a mallet and chisel. They were fastened together using wooden pegs called "treenails" for a tight, sturdy fit that avoids the use of metal bolts, brackets, nails, or other fasteners.

Mimicking the surrounding trees, the cabin is sided with vertically oriented boards and battens. Inside, the handsome timbers with pegged joints and tapered braces are left exposed, emphasizing the strong, simple lines of the structure.

Although the walls are conventionally framed and insulated, the inside walls are finished with plasterboard and plaster instead of conventional drywall for a creamy, hand-rubbed appearance.

On the main level, the kitchen joins with sitting and dining areas, all centered around a wood-burning stove. The acid-washed concrete floor is hard-wearing, easy to maintain, and incorporates an efficient, floor-warming radiant-heat system. Warm in the winter, the floor is perfect for doors-open living with lots of pets.

Custom-built from recycled woods, the kitchen cabinets are painted white and apple green (see page 65). The light green visually helps cool some of the bright mountain sun, while cut-glass drawer pulls gleam like gems.

Upstairs, the bedroom nestles close beneath the massive rafters, the ceiling lofts over the living area below, and the sense of space and light is increased. In the bedroom, a handsome spruce floor and French doors open onto a sunny deck that connects the loftlike sleeping area with the outdoors.

The bathroom has a similar loft, plus an interior window that transmits light and affords privacy. An old-fashioned claw-foot tub and beaded-board paneling painted to match the kitchen cabinets give this room a vintage look.

1 Simple shapes, exposed structure, and board-and-batten siding evoke the feel of a barn, a fitting look for this cabin that's perched on the edge of a small clearing in the woods.

2 A sturdy stoop and a custom-built door welcome visitors to this quaint Colorado cottage that blends into its setting.

1 An interior window next to the claw-foot tub is sandblasted to a frosty translucence, allowing the bath to share light with the rooms below it while retaining privacy.

2 A vaulted ceiling, hand-plastered plain white walls, and windows make the diminutive first floor sparkle. The floor is durable dyed concrete.

3 French doors drench the loft bedroom in sunshine and lead to a treetop deck. Spruce floors, a peeled-pole bed frame, and a vintage table and chair add to the rustic charm of the room.

4 Windows in the kitchen run extra tall to maximize light; cool green cabinetry exudes a sense of cool and calm.

Small Package
Dream House

980 sq.ft.

A compact, traditionally styled house with nearly equal amounts of indoor and outdoor living space is cozy for one—and perfect for a crowd. It was intended to serve as temporary quarters for the homeowner while she purchased adjoining land on which to build a 2,800-square-foot dream home. Along the way she discovered that the small quarters suited her lifestyle perfectly, and she settled in for good.

This one-level, four-room house makes a cozy home for one or two. One roof over the house and another over the screen porch make for varied rooflines that are attractive outside and allow 18-foot-high vaulted ceilings within. The high ceilings increase the diminutive home's volume and create a sense of spaciousness. A large bookcase separates the bedroom and living room, and a partial wall defines the kitchen, providing an open floor plan whose long sight lines trick the eye into thinking the house is much larger than it is.

Despite the high ceilings and open floor plan, this house is traditional in character. Architectural details such as trim, windows, and dark parquet floors join furnishings and artwork to create a home that is big on sophistication.

Entertaining small groups or large gatherings of 75 or more is easy to do here. In addition to the screen porch off the kitchen, a pergola-topped brick patio stretches across one exterior wall, offering nearly as much living space outdoors as there is inside.

The home's attractive landscaping—brick paths and patio, broad lawn, and mature trees—give the little house a sense of stature and grace that belies its diminutive size.

3

4

1 The pergola-topped brick patio serves as the home's front entry. A curving stone path draws foot traffic toward the house.

2 The house is sited to maximize sunlight from the east, west, and south. To the north, cypress trees obscure the view of houses nearby.

3 Crown molding rims the kitchen cabinets, giving the space a finished, intimate look. The molding and cabinet-top lighting lead the eye up to the pottery collection and vaulted ceiling.

4 Beneath a pavilion-style roof and vaulted ceiling, a screen porch makes living outdoors easy.

1 In the living room, French doors with muntined transom windows and sidelights open the entire wall to the patio beyond.

2 A partial wall separates the living room from the kitchen. Overhead, unobtrusive track lighting mounts on trusses that cross the vaulted ceiling of tongue-and-groove paneling.

3 The home's lone bathroom is an attractive and hardworking place. It includes linen closets, a washer and dryer, and a pullout clothesline.

4 Dark-stained parquet floors ground the vaulted spaces so the feeling is expansive yet anchored. In the bedroom, a simple scheme of cream backdrops—bedding, draperies, and walls—and dark case goods and flooring are warmed with just a few amber- and copper-hued throws and pillows.

Clean and Simple

2,071 sq.ft.

Straightforward and unfussy, this house is designed for an indoor-outdoor lifestyle thoughtfully arranged to create a maximum of living space. Another 1,000 square feet is ready for development in the basement.

Built in Michigan in a wooded neighborhood of older houses, this freshly built home is designed to blend in. A double front porch, batten trim, stained cedar siding, and a brick chimney complement the surrounding neighbors.

Outdoor living spaces claim three sides of the house: a screen porch off the dining room, a sunroom off the kitchen, and a deck nestled between the sunroom and garage. In addition, one porch extends from the living room and another from the master suite above it.

Inside, the U-shape kitchen, open to public spaces on two sides, anchors the home. Half-walls on the kitchen's U-arms keep messes from public view and are topped with shelflike ledges for greater utility. The cook can see nearly the entire first floor—even the fire crackling in the living room hearth.

4 5

Exposure *Notes*

The southeastern exposure of the deck and sunroom make them prime locations for enjoying the sunrise. The southern exposure warms the sunroom in the chill of winter.

The screen porch has a northwestern exposure, giving it the best view of setting sunsets.

When foliage fills in over summer, the upper level has the best panoramic view. The entire house was elevated 3 feet to gain this perspective.

1 Wide mulched beds of trees, shrubs, and grasses suit the woodsy setting.

2 The sunroom's southern orientation means it is always warm and cozy, even in winter.

3 Topped with a curved counter, a half-wall at the kitchen peninsula forms a snack bar. The bar also conceals kitchen clutter from the dining room.

4 The house offers two ways to enjoy the woods in back: The deck is a popular choice when mosquitoes aren't a problem; when bugs prevail, the sunroom serves with screened windows wide open to catch the breezes or closed for warmth.

5 The kitchen's U-shape forms an efficient "cooking cockpit." It's open to the sunroom and deck on one side, the dining room on another.

6 To keep the garage from blocking woodland views on either side of the house, it's placed behind and to the side of the utility rooms.

6

Lower Level

Main Level

Second Level

71

1

2

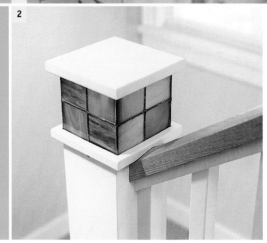

Curves and Other Smart Moves This home includes a variety of inventive details. Some add visual interest; some reduce maintenance and further comfort.

Curved ledges make up the fireplace mantel and are repeated in kitchen and bath countertops.

Porch railings are designed to shed moisture from rain and snow. Rather than using flat rails, these rails feature a 5-degree bevel to create a slope for runoff.

A lighted newel post and tubular skylight illuminates the stairwell. A mirror in the stairwell (not shown) is framed and trimmed to match the windows upstairs.

1 Old croquet balls wedged between two curved shelves create a distinctive yet inexpensive fireplace mantel. On the floor, laminated oak handles the wear and tear it gets from active family pets.

2 A stained-glass cap slips over a lighted newel post, creating a pretty guide light in the stairwell at night.

3 French doors in the master bedroom open to a small outdoor balcony.

4 The star of this simple dining room is the view of the woods outside. French doors open to a screen porch.

2,300 sq.ft.

A smart layout and a combination of cozy and open spaces create a house that's sized perfectly—both for intimate family life and big convivial gatherings.

Just the Right Size

This charismatic house feels big, yet at 2,300 square feet it's quite compact by any standard. Add up all its features, amenities, and you'd be surprised that it fits into such a modest footprint.

Walk through the front door and there's a comfortable library to the side. Beyond the library, a wide-open living and dining area spills out French doors that lead to the back of the yard.

An L-shape wall separates the kitchen from the living areas, but cooks have no trouble conversing with family and guests in the dining room through a large window. The kitchen island and banquette provide plenty of room for chatting and gathering. A first floor laundry adjacent to the kitchen makes juggling domestic tasks convenient.

The second level has more cubic space than it may appear from the exterior, because of large gables. It boasts two bedrooms, a bath, plenty of storage, and room for expansion. This floor is designed to handle the family's changing needs and can handily become another gathering space or larger home office.

1

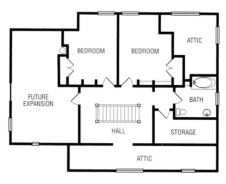

2

Main Level

3

Second Level

1 Cottage style details—window boxes, muntined windows, blue shudders, and shake shingles—are scaled small for a cozy look

2 Landscaping is simple now; the lot's slight slope lends itself to a stepped down patio or deck later.

3 This home was designed for a family of four, but it's roomy enough for more. The first floor master suite and laundry cater to one-level living when kids and visitors move on.

4 Light flows freely from living room to dining area. Subtle touches, such as the birch-faced ceiling beam, define the two spaces. The window seat is modeled after one that appeared in a 1905 Scandinavian folk art book.

5 The living room faces north, but the wood-burning fireplace keeps it toasty warm.

6 White trim and flower boxes brighten the exterior. Diamond cutouts adorn the shutters.

7 White stair rails recall the Scandinavian heritage of the homeowners.

75

1 2

When You're the General Contractor

Being your own general contractor is a challenge. The more you can prepare yourself for the job, the better off you'll be. Here are some tips to get you started:

Allow yourself time. It's a full-time job, not something that can be done in the evenings. Plan to be up early every day calling everyone who will work on the house that day. Count on visiting the site daily to meet with contractors.

Keep a calendar. Note when all the subcontractors and inspectors need to be present. Map out how long each job (such as framing, roofing, or plumbing) should take, adding seven or eight days to each effort to allow for weather issues and ordering delays.

Do some work yourself. To cut costs and make your dream home more affordable, fill waste receptacles and complete end-of-day cleanup tasks yourself. You can also handle such tasks as applying exterior shingles, finishing drywall, painting, and staining.

See "Be Your Own General Contractor" on page 182 for more information.

3

1 A pass-through over the sink allows conversation to flow between kitchen and dining room.

2 Snugged into a three-window bay, the banquette is easy to get in and out of.

3 Pale-painted paneling covers two thirds of the dining room walls. Hanging artwork below the paneling ledge positions it for table-height viewing.

4 Paneled wainscoting in a bedroom is an inexpensive way to add instant detail to a room.

5 The tiny off-white and blue bathroom tiles form a challenging Greek key pattern.

4

5

Farm-Style
Suburban

2,460 sq.ft.

Rooms other than great-rooms can supply light and airy ambience. This modern-day farmhouse offers distinct living spaces that are open to one another.

Here's a house that breaks two common tenets of conventional wisdom. One, you *can* have comfy farmhouse style in a freshly built suburban house; and two, all new houses don't have to have great-rooms.

This new house is just one in a new neighborhood of similarly styled homes. It blends the best of Victorian-era farmhouse style with a distinctive floor plan that is neither wide open nor compartmentalized. Washed in an energizing color palette, the home's appeal is inarguable, whether it sits in a rural or urban setting. On the first floor, a combination of half-walls and columns defines the living spaces. Trim, from windows to railings, is simple and traditionally styled. Painted white, it adds dimension to the walls and keeps the look light. Although the floor plan appears to ramble, by positioning front and back entries and the central staircase near one another, little space is lost to a hallway. Upstairs, the master bedroom takes advantage of angles common in Victorian architecture, gaining a vaulted ceiling beneath the roof pitch. The effect? It's like a tree-top aerie.

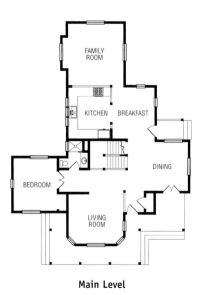

Main Level

Upper Level

3

4

1 A steeply pitched roof, wraparound porch, and simple exterior ornament suggest an old Victorian farmhouse, yet this is a freshly built suburban home.

2 From the entry, one can see the living room, dining room, and breakfast area. Half-walls and paint colors define the rooms.

3 Throw open the French doors, and gatherings of family and friends can flow freely from the dining room to the porch.

4 Columns and crown moldings define the kitchen work core, which opens to the breakfast room. White-painted woodwork keeps the hefty columns from visually dominating the small spaces.

79

1 A U-shape kitchen is highly efficient. Here, white cabinets, trim, and appliances create a fresh look that complements the adjoining rooms' celery green hue. Collectibles perch on crown moldings.

2 Classic pedestal sinks flank a dresserlike, tile-topped vanity in the master bath. An interior window above the vanity borrows light from the adjacent bedroom.

3 A wall niche is perfectly sized for a dresser, leaving plenty of uninterrupted floor space. In the same way mellow cream cuts the bitter taste of coffee, the bedroom's soft green color takes the edge off the bright sunlight that otherwise might overpower the bedroom.

2

3

81

A Simple
Beauty

2,095 sq.ft.

Beneath a tentlike roofline, through-views and smart placement of gathering and private spaces clear the way for a big-space, open living.

This home was built within an existing neighborhood of older, small homes and few new houses, so its exterior design is purposefully unpretentious. The facade is simple and traditional, while the home's clean lines give it a modern aesthetic. Tentlike center gables and circular windows at the front and back peaks pinpoint public areas—the living and dining rooms and kitchen. Smaller sections flanking the gables shelter private zones: a master bedroom, bath, and office on one side; children's bedrooms and bath and a laundry on the other. Arbors set into the roofline and gable windows and doors align for through-views, making the most of natural light and helping the home live like a larger space.

The front entry opens onto the gathering spaces. A band of checker-board-painted hardwood floor stretches across the entry, a visual hallway leading to the private spaces at either end. The kitchen is defined with beaded-board cabinetry; staggered tops keep the cooking area from feeling block-like. Some of the cabinetry is painted rose color; some is stained to blend with the room's furnishings. Two-sided glass cabinets obscure the view into the kitchen from the entry but light sparkles through. In the living room, a stone hearth, built-in shelves and

Taming *Tall Walls*

When the walls stretch to the roof peak, as they do in this home, the resulting expanse of flat wall space can seem overwhelming. To bring the surface more appeal, the walls, *left*, feature a grid of medium-density fiberboard battens. The grid starts in 6-foot squares near the top of the ceiling, finishing in 3-foot squares just above windows and doors to bring the massive surface down to scale. In the home office, *above*, built-in shelving runs clear up to the ceiling line, offering a wealth of storage.

1 *See-through views are created by lining up windows and doors on both sides of the house. Here, you can see through the round accent windows beneath the peak, the ground-level windows, and double doors. The technique creates a spacious, open feel in any home.*

2 *Beneath coats of wall paint, a continuous grid of flat trim pieces subtly break up the expanses of wall space in the open living, kitchen, and dining space.*

3 *Facing the living room, three doors on the rose-painted cabinets open to 8-inch shelves. The fourth door is false, forming the end of the tall perpendicular cabinet run. The brushed stainless-steel footrest at the snack bar is a nice comfort feature.*

cabinets, and a tongue-and-groove pine ceiling combine for warm and cozy ambience. To balance the budget, special features in the sleeping areas were restrained. The master bedroom, for example, has a simple pair of closets rather than a walk-in, plus built-in drawers and a TV niche.

A front courtyard and porch, a back deck and patio, and a side garden make it easy to spend an afternoon outdoors. The shaded courtyard is a cool and comfortable hangout when high winds or hot sun blast the home's more exposed backyard.

Main Level

1

1 Free-form concrete pavers ease the transition from the deck to the fire pit and landscaped beds. A few well-placed round windows conjure nautical images.

2 A window seat at the hallway end beckons sitters to stop and enjoy the garden view. The cushioned seat lifts for access to storage below.

3 Separate twin vanities with a shallow chest between them bypass a conventional look in the master bath.

3

4 A vaulted ceiling helps create the illusion of a voluminous master bedroom.

2

Scandinavian
Country Cottage

2,600 sq.ft.

Combining old-world style with super insulated comfort, this cottage mixes traditional timber-frame craftsmanship with the strength, quiet, and warmth of structural insulated panels.

This enchanting home offers a flexible floor plan with cozy spaces for family and an easygoing openness for entertaining. Ample porches, windows, and decks reach out for sunshine and views; inside, Scandinavian country design is softly colorful and soothing.

Structurally the house mixes centuries-old post-and-beam construction with state-of-the-art wall and roof panels. The combination is strong enough to allow soaring open spaces inside and efficient enough to keep the house comfortable in extreme climate conditions without causing substantial heating and cooling costs.

At the home's core, a great-room rises among towering timbers. Knee braces arch from the timbers to support roof beams. The result is a look that's like a forest of branches set against the ceiling's pale blue sky.

The great-room encompasses five distinct areas: a formal entry separated from the central living room by a see-through fireplace wall; the living room itself, defined by a carpeted floor and cozy seat-

1 *This inviting cottage exudes old-world ambience from the first step through the door with beaded-board walls, a vinyl floor that has a Scandinavian-check pattern, and the balcony's decorative cutout detailing. Wall sconces flank a fireplace that's shared with the living room.*

2 *A simple fireplace and chimney—inexpensively created with dimension lumber, stock molding, beaded board, and drywall—separate the living room from the foyer.*

ing centered around the hearth; an efficient kitchen (with island) to the right; a sitting area to the left; and a dining area opposite the entry. A porch off the entry and two decks, one each off the sitting and dining areas, set the scene for indoor-outdoor entertaining and dining.

The private spaces fill in the corners: a master bedroom and spacious master bath, a guest bedroom with its own bath, and an office with a powder room. The design is incredibly flexible; the master bath and office could just as well serve as additional bedrooms or as hobby or studio spaces.

Frame-and-Panel Construction

Post-and-beam construction (in which vertical posts and horizontal beams carry a structure's weight, rather than the walls themselves) had been around for centuries before the first load-bearing 2x4 stud wall was erected. Buildings from the post-and-beam era stand testament to that method's durability. It is also an adaptable technique that allows open space. Another plus is that post-and-beam homes boast a rare beauty; whitewashed or natural, their massive timbers are magnificent.

New technologies enhance timber framing's timeless appeal. Foam-core wall and roof panels—commonly called Structural Insulated Panels or SIPs, can cross long spans, facilitating soaring ceilings and open floor plans in homes with or without a timber-frame armature. The panels are typically made of large sheets of rigid foam insulation sandwiched between panels of structural plywood or Oriented Strand Board (a plywoodlike panel made of wood chips that have been glued together under high pressure). SIPs are incredibly strong—an advantage in areas where homes are subject to heavy snows, tornadoes, earthquakes, or hurricanes. The panels have high insulation values too, creating homes that are quiet and energy-efficient. The panels are resource-efficient, too, requiring less wood per foot of wall than does stud-wall construction. Finally, they can be made with a prefinished interior panel—such as beaded-board plywood—simplifying and speeding construction.

Construction speed is a major advantage of frame-and-panel homes, which are generally pre-engineered at a factory, then erected on site. This home was assembled in just seven days inside Minnesota's Mall of America by *Better Homes and Gardens Country Home* magazine to showcase advances in home-building technology.

For more information see "Alternative Building Materials," page 185.

1 2

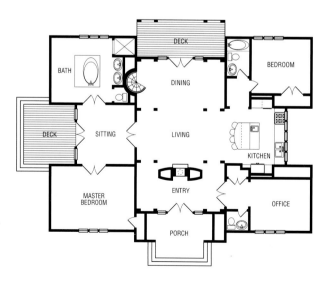

Main level

3
4

1 A long trestle table and simple white-painted chairs are lit by a graceful wrought-iron chandelier in the dining alcove. The spiral stairway ascends to a balcony and storage area; the French doors lead to a deck outside.

2 A lofty ceiling with dormer windows at its peak floods the living room with light; the kitchen alcove has a matching bank of glass. Sunny yellow walls and white-washed oak timbers add to the cheerful ambience.

3 Black and white flooring and polished chrome fixtures give the master bath an elegant edge. The pristine environment features an inviting whirlpool tub in the center of the room.

4 The view into the sitting room from the master suite deck reveals a transition of gentle colors into the greatroom and kitchen beyond. From this perspective, the master bedroom is to the right, and the bath to the left, of the sitting room.

Building a home on a steep hillside lot with strict roofline and tree-protection ordinances is never a simple matter. Here, the solution is a kite-shape floor plan with a low roofline and dramatic angles.

An Angle Called Home

To those who prize expansive views and a thickly wooded home base, a lot's 6-foot grade change is simply part of what makes a site magical. The home built on this lot had to incorporate the grade change as well as ordinances that severely restrict building height and tree removal. The architect home-owner responded with a kite-shape, two-level house that celebrates its setting. An open floor plan that capitalizes on indoor-outdoor relationships, glass, and natural materials creates a warm, contemporary Craftsman style that's also heavily influenced by Frank Lloyd Wright. In perfect harmony with its site, the new house is stunning, but the wooded setting is the star.

While square houses are more economical to build, a home full of angles possesses an elegance all its own and does not require expensive detailing. Angled spaces often appear larger than they really are and draw the eye through the home. Here, light wells and clerestory windows ensure each room has plenty of natural light. Light fixtures recessed into dropped ceiling soffits are unobtrusive until they're needed at night. Built-in storage and display shelves throughout the home eliminate the need for bulky furnishings. In keeping with Craftsman and Wrightian principles, the home's character comes from a blend of woods and other hardy, natural materials. Redwood siding wraps the exterior. Inside, oak floors, Douglas fir ceilings, mahogany doors, and teak built-ins reign. In the kitchen, a granite countertop rests on cabinets of cherry-banded maple.

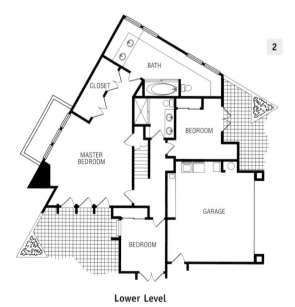
1

2

Lower Level

1 Massive windows revealing woodsy views flank the living room's brick fireplace. The hearth's copper-hooded design is intentionally simple, so that outdoor drama becomes the room's primary ornament.

2 Outdoor living spaces are essential to this home. Patios flow from two of the three bedrooms on the lower level; a deck stretches into the trees on the upper level.

3 The kitchen celebrates natural materials with clean-lined cabinets in maple banded with cherry, granite countertops, and hardwood floors. Trapezoid-shape windows above the cabinets draw the eye to the vaulted ceiling and treetop views.

4 A trapezoid front door opens to the dining and living room. To gain both light and privacy, the front door is fitted with pebbled glass. Just inside the door, a built-in angled hutch is one of many features that underscore the home's angle motif.

91

1 2
3

1 *Because parking is on the lower level, a curved stucco wall with planters calls guests up a short flight of stairs to the front door.*

2 *To extend the home's living space, a large deck stretches off the den and into the woods. The heavy railing style is necessary given the slope that it sits over.*

3 *Part of the roof structure is left open to pull light into the north interior.*

4 *Visitors encounter the home's angle again at the countertop in the main-level powder room off the entry.*

5 *Awning windows draw light and breezes into the master bath. The tiled tub surround creates a privacy wall for the toilet.*

4
5

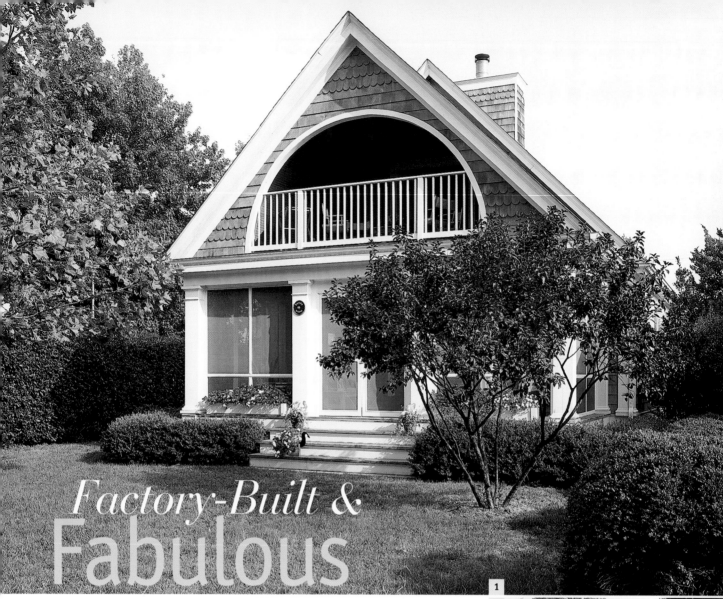

Factory-Built & Fabulous

1,700 sq.ft.

Designed by its architect-owner and built in a factory, this Delaware summer cottage is an inspiring charmer. Its porch and shingled exterior complement nearby vintage neighbors, but its construction is cutting-edge.

Though this summer house is notable for its good looks—graceful white columns, crisp trim, and barrel-vaulted porch roof—it's equally noted for its construction. Built in a factory, the house arrived on site via two flatbed trucks. The pieces were then lifted off and set up, resulting in a fully completed home in six days. It's a house that undermines any notion that factory-built houses are boxy, boring, or architecturally insignificant.

The size, shape, and rooflines of this house complement neighboring cottages. It even includes the local requisite delight—a front screen porch. The home's special features continue. Rows of square-cut cedar shingles are accented with three-row bands of fish-scale shingles. Beneath the steeply pitched roof, a barrel-vaulted ceiling forms an upper-level porch accessible from an interior stairway. The unique porch shape is a visual treat whether seen from the street or from beneath its sheltering curve.

To afford quality, most of the budget went to the home's exterior and public rooms. The kitchen is attractive rather than lavish, with stock cabinets pickled in cream tones

and topped with laminate counters. Lower-level bedrooms—easy to upgrade later—are spare and simple. Upstairs, the porch is finished and functional, while the bedroom spaces will be finished later to become a master suite.

1 A main-level screen porch topped with an upper-level porch offers street-side options for outdoor living.

2 The roofline and shape of this home were planned to complement neighboring houses. The detailed lap siding and barrel-shape upper porch add touches of distinction.

3 With two finished bedrooms on the main level, the two bedrooms upstairs are unfinished until budget allows.

Postponing some finish work is a smart move when you want to get into a property but don't need to use all the square footage immediately.

4 The cottage's floor plan includes four bedrooms and three full baths. Some of the sleeping rooms easily transform to serve office, fitness, or media needs. The homeowners plan to finish the upstairs as a skylit master suite, with the bedroom to the back and a sitting area with a fireplace to the front.

5 The barrel-vaulted ceiling throws a delightful curve into the upper porch and adds interest and shape to the home. Details, such as the ceiling's stained beaded-board surface and parquetlike floor, add further visual delight. The floor is covered with prefabricated decking squares purchased at a home center.

Main Level   **Upper Level**

4

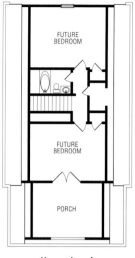

5

1

2

1 In this house, no public room is cut off from the other. Here, the dining room is adjacent to the cozy living area and is separated from the kitchen by only a peninsula.

2 A U-shape, cockpitlike kitchen lay-out makes quick, efficient work of meal preparation. The standard birch cabi-nets are pickled and fitted with simple, wipe-clean ceramic knobs.

3 A pair of French doors open the front screen porch to the interiors, expanding the living areas. The flat ceiling is covered with the same stained beaded board that covers the barrel vaulted ceiling of the top porch above.

4 The living room's gas fireplace cozies the main living area and creates a focal point for furnishings. Book-shelves and cabinetry on one side of the hearth are balanced by a doorway on the other.

A Smart *Choice*

If you still think of modular homes as boxy little things, it's time to dust off that idea and get an update. Modular homes are built in pieces in the shelter of a factory, then delivered and fit together on-site. They're becoming an increasingly savvy home-building construction choice. Modular home companies offer a vast array of home plans and employ architects who can assist in modifying them. Many companies also build to plans that you or your architect supplies. Factories eliminate weather-related downtime and offer assembly-line efficiency and quality control, so modular houses tend to cost less and take less time to construct than do site-built counterparts. Many houses can be built within 45 days, then finished on-site within 7 to 90 days. Site-built houses, on the other hand, can require 4 to 12 months from start to finish.

Modular is an excellent choice when favorable weather or affordable labor is in short supply. As for quality, factory-built houses are constructed to withstand the rigors of shipping, so they're generally built more precisely and are often more sturdy and durable than site-built structures. Don't overlook the idea of modular additions, which come with the same time- and cost-saving benefits as do complete houses. For more information see "Your Systems-Built Home, Modular" on page 54.

3

4

Making Your Room *Great*

Part family fun zone, part entertaining space, and part home theater, a great-room plays many roles. Since those roles can conflict, good planning is a must. Look beyond the space printed on your plan to develop activity zones that help you balance the action. To simplify the process, you might want to bring in an interior designer before construction begins.

Find Focus

If two activities or focal points compete, such as the fireplace and television, give each equal treatment—and maybe even its own zone. Some homeowners prefer having these pieces side by side; placing them on walls that face each other or on adjacent, angled walls is an appealing alternative. Chairs mounted on swivels can be helpful. Plan for adequate shades or draperies on the windows to prevent glare on the TV screen.

Plan Activity Spaces

If your family will do more in your great-room than watch a fire or TV program, make room for it. Book-

shelves and comfy conversation areas, plus surfaces for homework, paying bills, and playing games all can be built in, eliminating the need for space-gobbling furnishings.

Tie the Combo

The consistent use of built-ins can unite activity areas with a common look. Review the great-room plans on this page with an eye to multi-function and effective arrangements.

1 This great-room pulls seating into a floating arrangement, with features that hug the walls. A built-in corner cabinet with retractable pocket doors houses the TV and sound equipment. Across the room, a desk space facilitates paperwork. Seating is grouped around the fireplace, but swivel-mounted chairs are easy to turn to the TV. A window seat and bookshelves serve a reader when shades aren't dropped to reduce screen glare. Traffic flows around the seating group; there's little reason for anyone to walk in front of TV viewers or those who are fireside.
2 Here's another arrangement, with furnishings that ring the room. Folks stretched out on the L-shape sofa can enjoy either the fireplace or the TV. A desk initiates the shelving components that stretch from around the TV and past the fireplace to create a book nook. The short end of the sofa is near the kitchen, where a counter is ready to serve snacks.
3 A thick trim headband unites the fireplace niche with the television across angled, adjacent wall planes. Window views play a supporting role.

A Foyer Sets the Stage

1

Your home's foyer is a guest's introduction to your home—your own "welcome home" each time you step through the door. As you fine-tune your house plans, think about the message you want to send. Whether you go with a cozy greeting or a grand two-story entrance, you need to balance both theatrical and practical aspects. Three-story foyers with marble floors can feel like a museum and steal too much space from upper floors. Likewise, a too-small foyer is cramped and problematic when groups arrive, not to mention making you feel as if you're ducking into a cave. Rule of thumb? Don't sacrifice square footage at the entry if you can help it. Use these ideas and perspectives when evaluating potential foyer arrangements:

Let architectural style lead the foyer design. Avoid introducing a design element—window shape or door style—that doesn't relate to anything else in your home.

Preserve mystery and privacy by obscuring a complete view of the house from the foyer.

Build anticipation with a sight line to a focal point such as a window with a backyard view or a staircase.

Fill it with light by using sidelights or transom windows and interior light fixtures.

Shape it into a rotunda or hexagon.

Define the foyer with special flooring or a step up or step down into the rest of the house.

Ease the transition from outdoors to indoors with dropped ceiling beams or by extending a soffit or shelf.

Boost function with closets and hooks, a bench for setting packages and removing shoes, and a small table for keys and mail.

Add personality with a favorite painting or collected work.

Avoid having a front door open directly onto a blank wall, staircase, closet, or powder room.

1 Curves, simple columns, and geometry make an artful entry here. Leaded-glass doors and glass-block windows above draw in light; a limestone and marble floor complements the wood beams, railings, and ironwork.

2 A pair of French doors flanked and topped by windows create a bright, welcoming foyer. When open, the turquoise exterior door adds a splash of color against pale taupe walls and white and unstained trim. The chandelier hints at the homeowner's personal style.

3 Drawing the eye to the loftlike upper level, the staircase beyond is the focal point of this clean-lined, angled entry. A step up and a change in flooring material, from blue tile to hardwood, marks the transition from foyer to living room.

4 In a formal home with an open, vaulted plan, a foyer takes shape with three round columns topped with an entablature. The sight line crosses the living room to a wall of glass overlooking the backyard.

5 Several features distinguish the foyer in this Craftsman-inspired home: from hand-crafted cabinetry and bench that separate the entry from the dining space to the handsome tile and wood inlay on the floor.

6 Sunshine streams through sidelights flanking the pine front door to set this entry's yellow stucco walls aglow. A simple stair railing and concrete floor are part of the foyer, which is roomy enough for coat hooks, a chair, and a dresser. Striking accents—a coral rug and a tile headband above the door—set a vibrant mood.

Window Wise

W indows are one of your new home's most important elements. They are functional, allowing necessary ventilation and emergency escape, and they possess immense potential for adding character and drama to your house. A well-designed window plan can make your home appear larger and more spacious. If you arrange your windows for successive through-views, so no matter where you stand your eye is drawn through your home to a lovely view, you'll never feel hemmed in, regardless of the square footage beneath your feet. Window quality and pleasing design boost a home's feel-good factor immediately and add to its value for years to come.

Window Shopping

Windows become more efficient every decade. Low-emissivity (low-

E) and ultraviolet (UV) coatings, and double- and triple-pane glass with gas filling reduce heat transfer and block fabric-fading rays. Construction improvements make windows that tilt in for cleaning. On top of those features, the U.S. Environmental Protection Agency's Energy Star Program recommends windows with low U-factor (or high R-values) in areas where homes are heated much of the year, and low solar heat coefficients (SHGC) in climates that require frequent air-conditioning. Airtightness is another important measure; a rating of .2 is good, .1 or lower is best. This information is easy to find. The National Fenestration Rating Council's (NFRC) labeling program makes sure all this information is on window labels.

Design Tips

Windows reinforce and complement your home's architecture. They're expensive, and you can't change them as easily as you can, for example, a wall with an inexpensive coat of paint. When choosing and placing windows, don't overindulge and try to find as many ways as you can to reveal a glimpse of your property. You can still give your house plenty

of wow factor, but plan your window themes and stick to them throughout the house. Variations should relate to the overall style and share more than one design aspect, such as length, shape, number, and size of divided lights.

Go for long sight lines, also known as through-views, such as a view from the foyer through the house to the back room's hearth or from the kitchen through a living area out to a garden.

Don't forget no-view windows. Interior transom windows, operable or fixed on top of windows or doors, boost the amount of light and air that flows through your home. Glass-block windows crafted in the same shape as your other windows can draw sparkling light into a room where privacy is an issue or where the view outdoors is less than stellar.

The Sun Protection Factor

You can play up your views with numerous windows, but too much exposure to the west and south can be a drawback. After you whittle your design options to a few, study the number of windows exposed to the sun without trees or porches to break up the rays. A good rule for western exposures, for example, is to

4

limit the amount of glass in a wall's total surface area to no more than 50 percent. If you're looking at more, keep the ceiling height in a two-story exposed living space to 12 feet, which still offers plenty of volume. Another solution is to build a porch, open or enclosed, with deep overhangs to limit the light but allow the view. A third solution is to place the view in a lesser-used living space that's wide open to rooms farther away from the heat.

3

1 *Sloping lots provide homeowners plenty of opportunities to capitalize on a view. This home takes advantage of hills and valleys beyond with two walls of windows. Deep roof overhangs keep the room from getting too hot.*

2 *A covered porch with mesh railings admits a full view of the lush ravine beyond and keeps the interior cool.*

3 *Two windows abutting one another from adjacent staircase walls form a corner view overlooking a pretty patio and nearby wetlands.*

4 *A combination of square windows underscores this bedroom's contemporary geometric style. Fixed windows are easy on the budget; three of the lower windows are operable for pulling in a breeze.*

Built-In Functional Character

It's possible to add storage space to your home without adding square footage. At the same time you can infuse your home with character, distinction, and more value. How? Simply include smart built-in features. Well-executed built-ins are a surefire means of boosting your home's efficiency *and* personality quotient. They help you free up floor space and reduce the need for stand-alone furniture by slipping beds, collection displays, and things like bookshelves into lengths, wedges, and slivers of space.

One way to look for built-in opportunities is to examine your house plan for unused pieces of space—beneath eaves, under staircases, along blank walls. You can easily drywall the interior of an unused space and fit it with shelves. You can also fit those spaces with doors, drawers, or architectural trim that appears elsewhere in your home.

Another way to look for built-in opportunities is to think of them as "built-outs," structures that create niches, bookshelves, or partial walls that further shape open space. In most cases, you should work with a designer who honors the design motifs you have established for your house. Doing so will boost the impact of the built-ins and the long-term appeal of your home. For example, if your home is contemporary and free of architectural trim, stick with that clean-lined theme. If arches and divided light windows dominate, bring those features to your bookcases and niches.

1 Tucked into a niche under a steeply pitched roof, this bed offers cozy accommodations with no loss of floor space. The gentle arch repeats those in the home's passageways. The niche bed is a good solution if a guest bedroom gets nixed in favor of a home office.

2 The otherwise wasted space beneath a staircase is transformed into a handsome storage feature.

3 Three short shelves ideal for books, pottery, or travel mementos back into a stairway landing.

4 Stained green, an attractively crafted mudroom organizer built into a corner keeps gear corralled yet visible and within reach. This piece is a "built-out," and it's topped with trim that mimics the room's crown molding.

5 Why block the view? Cleverly crafted cabinets and windows turn ordinary kitchen storage into architectural works of art.

6 Line a long hallway with drawers and cabinets for a feature you'll never regret. Shallow cabinets hold canned goods; deeper closets swallow scads of outerwear and oversize items; a lighted niche becomes a place for messages, mail, and keys. This one is made with stock cabinet doors and parts.

Cape Cod to the Front

3,367 sq.ft.

An unpretentious story-and-a-half front facade camouflages the three-story drama to the back. The floor plan was arranged with entertaining in mind.

Sloping lots offer a chance to indulge dual design personalities. The front of the house sits on the high side of this property, presenting a story-and-a-half Cape Cod-style facade to the street. The main entrance admits you to the home's upper-level foyer and a family room that reaches skyward beneath vaulted ceilings. Floor-to-ceiling windows pull guests toward the family room and its fabulous woodland view. Bedrooms on the second level, which open onto the foyer and family room below, are positioned at the home's front and sit over the main-level study and dining room, which fill out the front of the home.

The kitchen, breakfast room, and screen porch open to the main-level family room. Party guests like to mingle here before heading outdoors to enjoy more of the woods from the second-level deck beyond the kitchen. The deck features a dining and covered grill area and a flight of stairs down the yard's slope to flat ground, which abuts a golf course.

From the rear, the house is far more grand than its street-side face suggests. The ground level features mingling places, more floor-to-ceiling windows, and a basement walkout that's marked by French doors. The lower level bustles with activity: It includes an executive home office, an antiques refinishing studio, a game room, and yet another gathering room.

3

4

5

1 This classic Cape Cod exterior is crafted with synthetic fieldstone and fiber-cement siding that resists rot and termites. The porch features tongue-and-groove pressure-treated wood and real stone. At the front door, a rounded transom mimics the porch archway.

2 By pushing the screen porch and adjacent deck to the side of the house, family room views are unobstructed and the lower level's floor-to-ceiling windows are free of its darkening canopy.

3 The foyer and family room ceilings soar, punching through the second story. An upper-level hallway overlooks both rooms, which are in the middle of the house.

4 Square columns define the formal dining space. The front of the white built-in hutch is flush with the wall; its body pushes into the adjacent garage.

5 A pass-through window between the kitchen and the deck's covered grill area is a handy shortcut when dining outdoors. A ledge topped with solid-surface material makes it weather-resistant and sturdy.

Main Level

4

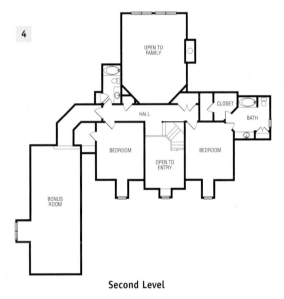

Second Level

5

1 In the family room, rounded windows stacked over double-hung units permit a floor-to-ceiling view of the trees.

2 With three exposed sides, the screen porch—located off the breakfast room—takes advantage of cooling breezes. A ceiling fan further stirs the air when needed.

3 The large kitchen caters to entertaining. In tighter quarters islands generally are located 3½ feet from base cabinets, but this one is pulled out a full 4 feet—enough for two people to pass easily during parties.

4 Finished portions of this house measure 3,367 square feet. The unfinished walk-out basement boasts 1,260 square feet and the unfinished bonus room, another 720 square feet.

5 The master bedroom's bay window celebrates backyard views; shutters are a gracious means of controlling light, privacy, and breezes. Uplighting tucked into the coffered ceiling soffits casts a soft glow at night.

2,720 sq.ft.

An L-shape stucco house hugs the side of its lot to make room for a courtyard and maximize indoor-outdoor living opportunities.

Sidestep
Solution

Many houses are plopped square in the middle of their lots. By contrast, this Southern California stucco hugs one side, making room for an extensive courtyard in the crook of the L-shape. The strategy works beautifully. Most rooms connect with the courtyard, making the entire house feel larger than it actually is.

The kitchen anchors the L-shape crook, sited so adults can supervise children in the pool. The walls that face the courtyard are predominantly glass doors and floor-to-ceiling windows that provide unobstructed views. The heavily used family room claims one side of the L; an office, dining room, and living room fill out the other. A second level tops the family side of the L with three bedrooms. All but one of the upstairs sleeping quarters face the water, and as a consolation, that one has a balcony.

1 *Galvanized roofing and wooden porch beams set a tropical scene. The home's unusual positioning maximizes the property's relax-and-play spaces, which include a sheltered courtyard, swimming pool, and gatehouse. Supervising outdoor activities from inside the house is easy—an important feature for a family with children.*

2 *The dividing line between indoors and out is blurred due to uniform tile pavers used throughout and a wall of windows and glass doors that open wide. It's easy to enjoy the outdoors no matter the weather on the covered patio that hugs the house, opening to the courtyard and pool area.*

3 *The home's plan includes three bedrooms upstairs and a guest bedroom and a den on the first floor. Currently the guest quarters serve as the pool bath. The office could easily become a bedroom if one-level living were desired.*

4 *Opposite the courtyard side of the kitchen, an outdoor cooking space gets plenty of use in the evenings. Features include a sink, grill, slate countertops, and a fireplace.*

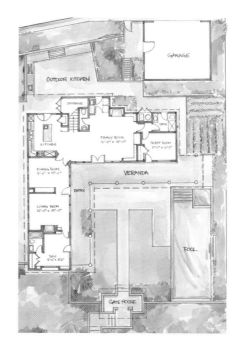

Gatehouse *Welcome*

Ocean views distinguish one side of this home's lot; the adjacent side faces a busy, noisy street front. A street-side courtyard wall and a gatehouse hugged by lush plantings solve privacy and entry issues. The homeowners use an intercom at the gatehouse to usher visitors into their courtyard and home. A garage sits at the back of the property and is accessed by an alley.

1 Paint-grade wood cabinetry and granite countertops featuring flecks of many colors give the kitchen decorative flexibility. Cabinets and walls are easily repainted and trim added.

2 French doors free of divided lights open onto the balcony in the master bedroom. Lush draperies that hang on a rod slide across when privacy or light control is needed.

3 Morning in this house generally starts with someone opening the family room wall of French doors to let breezes flow through. The family enjoys everyday meals at this table, close to the action between the kitchen and the courtyard.

4 A large footed tub in the master bath invites a soak. The nearby glass-block shower has a window to the courtyard.

5 Family and friends can relax in one of several seating areas or at the dining table in the shade of the patio roof.

6 Two pedestal sinks accompanied by a trio of vanities offer a unique solution to storage in the master bath.

3,705 sq.ft.

A 1930s-style bungalow with vintage interior details is shaped to fit a sloping lot and accommodate a big family and large gatherings.

This home shows that romantic architecture can be practical as well as pretty. Popular in the early decades of the 20th century (see "The American Bungalow" on page 117), the bungalow style offered suburbanites a romanticized version of the preindustrial country cottage with a look that retains its appeal today. This example also solves two contemporary situations: sloping lots (see "Slope Coping" on page 115) and large-scale entertaining of overnight guests. In fact, this house has five bedrooms—more per square foot than any other home in this book.

Three-level living was the key to meeting both challenges—and to creating a spacious home on a modest footprint. The main level is completely devoted to public spaces, with a single entry area accessed though both the front door and the garage. A hall leads past a half bath to a kitchen and dining area. That leaves the living room with a clear view of the backyard and access to a three-season porch.

Practical
Vintage

Upper Level

Main Level

Lower Level

1 *Sited on a lakeside lot, this spacious house retains the modest look of a vintage bungalow. Its low-sloping roof, centered dormer, porchlike deck, stone chimney, and porch piers are the picture of a quaint cottage. Inside, though, there's room for a crowd.*
2 *A cultured fieldstone fireplace serves as the focal point for the living room. The loft above is a game and TV room. Vertical strips of molding add a classic bungalow touch to the balcony half-wall.*
3 *The home's practical front entry provides storage for hats and coats and leads into a corridor that adjoins the kitchen, dining room, and living area. The built-in bench is handy for removing muddy shoes.*

An island cooktop separates the kitchen from the dining area. When guests and family members pitch in, the opposite side of the island becomes their work surface. The adjacent dining table seats eight, and three more find room at the island. Guests also spill into the adjoining living room, porch, and deck. The vast covered deck (it's wider than the house) serves as a large room in its own right. If insects invade the party, folks can adjourn to the screened patio directly below.

While open spaces and the living room's vaulted ceiling characterize the main level, the upper and lower levels are models of compact efficiency, sleeping a dozen or so people in five bedrooms and a bunk room. Such flexibility and capacity are ideal for this home's use as a vacation retreat, but the layout also makes a great primary residence for a large family.

Slope *Coping*

Picture a house designed for a sloping lot and you probably see a contemporary design with a walk-out basement fronted by sliding glass doors. The choices for such lots are vast, however, as this house proves. True, most traditional houses were designed for level lots, when land was plentiful in decades past and level sites easier to find. Fortunately many vintage designs are quite adaptable. This lakefront house retains its traditional bungalow look from both sides; it looks like a one-and-a-half story from the land side and a two-and-a-half story from the shore. To allow for maximum daylight and water views from even the lowest level, this home's builder carved into the land to get three sides of the house exposed, then terraced the 18-foot slope with limestone retaining walls.

1 Two-tone cabinetry adds vintage flavor to the kitchen. Dishes are easy to find stored on open shelving above the sink.

2 The dining area's custom built-in hutch looks as though it were handmade in the 1930s. Topped with a stainless-steel counter, it doubles as a serving buffet and stores linens and casual dinnerware.

3 These bunk beds were designed to fit in the smallest room on the lower level.

4 This loft space, above the dining area and open to the living area below, houses a pool table and TV. Two-foot-wide slate panels top the balcony half-wall, which doubles as a snack bar.

5 A flagstone path circles a simple front-yard garden. Steps lead to a concrete porch. This durable concrete material is stained the color of cedar to make it look warmer. The entry overhang's pier-and-column details match those on the lake side of the house.

6 Located just off the living area, this covered deck stretches the length of the house and provides a beautiful view of the lake. Plastic tongue-and-groove decking ensures a tight, insect-proof ceiling for the screened patio below.

The American Bungalow

Distinguished by their low horizontal profiles, front porches, and shallow-slope roofs, bungalows were first built in the late 1800s and reached the height of their popularity in the 1920s and '30s. As with Craftsman-style houses, the bungalow's simple design countered the highly ornamented Victorian houses that were popular in the preceding decades and reflected an effort to return to the simplicity of preindustrial times. Bungalows often feature:

• A front garden
• Simple front columns, often tapered and set on piers
• A front porch
• Cedar shingles
• Simple, flat-milled interior moldings, either painted or naturally finished
• Architectural details such as ceiling beams, roof brackets, and exposed rafter tails
• Built-in furnishings

5

6

117

1

rugated rustproof aluminum. Some of the metal is unfinished, some (inspired by a nearby patch of wildflowers) is painted deep yellow that contrasts nicely with the blue sky. The exposed portion of the walk-out basement echoes the scheme with some rows of concrete block left bare, some triple rows painted yellow. Up top, exposed white-painted rafter tails add to the home's casual flair. Inside the house, the corrugated metal theme continues in the kitchen, wrapping the back side of the curved island. Natural-finish birch floors in the house warm the industrial elements. While most of the interior furnishings are neutral, bold colors are purposefully used in the game room as a tie to the bold exterior hue.

The tall core of the house brings views and light to all three above-ground levels. The main-level entry opens onto the kitchen, the hub around which the dining, living, bar, deck, and game room spaces radiate. A deck wraps three sides of the main level. Simple railings are fitted with clear panels to block wind but not views. The third level contains a master suite with a sitting area and an office, all of which look onto the living area below. A roomy loft on the fourth level is an unfinished space ideal for a media room, art studio, or teen lounge. A small deck off the loft offers bird's eye views of the outdoors. Down under, the lower walk-out level features 9-foot ceilings, two bedrooms, a fitness room plus bath, sauna, and steam room. It opens onto a sheltered patio beneath the main-level deck.

2

3,700 sq.ft.

Useful living space is stacked on a boxy footprint in a modern house with a fresh look that's low-maintenance too.

This bright contemporary home graces the shoreline, although its plan makes sense on any lot where building tall—rather than wide—is necessary. That's often the case if you want to wedge a good-size home into a wooded area, a slope, or tiny lot.

A desire for low-maintenance materials drove exterior choices for this home. Siding and roofing is cor-

Clean
Contemporary

1 Floor-to-ceiling windows in the game area follow the pitch of the shed roof. When opened, the lower two rows of screened windows give the space a screen porch feel.

2 The stairs at the front of the house are stacked, an efficient use of floor space. Windows of diffusing glass and open stair treads keep the interior light.

3 Buttressing wings surround the home's tall center. East-facing windows draw sunlight into the house throughout the day.

4 Though the front door opens onto the kitchen, the kitchen has uninterrupted sight lines to the back of the home. Corrugated metal wraps the kitchen island, echoing the home's exterior cladding. Just around the bend of the kitchen island is the formal dining area. Groupings of conical pendant lamps supplement the recessed lighting.

5 The skylight concept extends to this overhang, which in most homes would be solid and thereby provide shade. Here, white corrugated fiberglass replaces lumber. Beneath it, the purlins and rafters are painted white, and the sun filters through.

6 From the kitchen, you can see through nearly every space in the house to the outdoors beyond. White birch upper cabinets fitted with reeded glass allow light to flow.

DECK

DECK | LIVING | DECK

BAR AREA | DINING

KITCHEN

GAME ROOM | ENTRY | LDRY

BATH

PORCH

Main Level

PATIO

BEDROOM | BATH | BEDROOM

SAUNA | STEAM

EXERCISE | HALL | LDRY/ MECH

Second Level

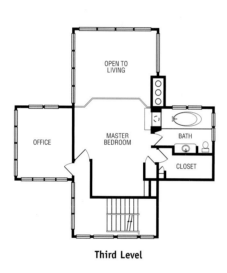

OPEN TO LIVING

OFFICE | MASTER BEDROOM | BATH

CLOSET

Third Level

LOFT

DECK

OPEN

Fourth Level

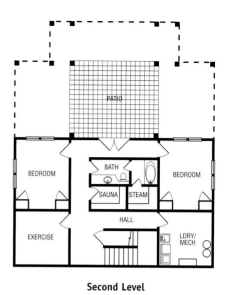

1 The master suite sitting area shares a two-sided gas fireplace with the master bath. Overlooking the living area below, the sitting area uses a railing with see-through lower panels beneath (not shown) to keep views clear.

2 In the living room, windows stretch up 20 feet to frame blue-sky views. Translucent shades—operated by remote control—drop to diffuse the light when needed. A gas fireplace anchors the limestone wall, which is purposefully stepped at the top, playing to the geometry of the windows.

1

2

FAMILY

KITCHEN

PTRY

DINING

PORCH

PORCH

LIVING

Main Level

BATH

BEDROOM

CLOSET

BATH

CLOSET

MASTER
BEDROOM

STUDY

Second Level

Gathering Home

3,631 sq.ft.

Styled with cottagelike architectural details, this house exudes warmth and comfort. An open kitchen flanked by family and dining rooms—each with a hearth—adds to the draw.

If your dream house is a big, comfortable open-door kind of place where everyone congregates after work, after the game, or before the wedding, take a look at this plan. Its design is based on the premise that everyone always gravitates to the kitchen. The kitchen anchors the home's open arrangement with a great-room on one side and a multi-purpose dining room on the other. Pillar-flanked islands delineate the kitchen space. A stone hearth in the great-room and a brick hearth in the dining room encourage family and friends to linger. Grouping an office, pantry wall, and staircase around the front door creates a foyer that shields the gathering spaces from full, immediate view. A mudroom, laundry, and powder room join the foyer to the three-car garage; you can also enter the rooms from the covered front porch.

Century-old cottages inspired the finish details here. A lower grade of pine was purposefully chosen for the great-room floor; its knots and nicks contribute to the casual vibe. River stones were chosen for their earthy quality, while new bricks used in the dining room fireplace and snack bar were tumbled to look like old pavers. The bricklayers even used a special tool to roughen the mortar so it, too, appears centuries old. On the walls, whitewashed planking is purposefully nailed together in a mismatched fashion.

Privacy is the focus upstairs. A long hallway intentionally separates entrances to the children's bedrooms from that of the master suite. Even better, the door to the master suite opens first to a bookshelf-lined alcove, which in turn opens onto the master bedroom.

1 This suburban house resembles a 1900s cottage. A mix of details, including river stones, shingles, and garage doors that appear to swing open, makes the look.

2 The roomy foyer's barnlike architectural details—pine-plank walls and flooring, iron hinges, and corner braces in the doorways—immediately establish a comfortable mood.

3 Pine-covered columns support the ceiling's whitewashed beams, visually separating the kitchen from the great-room and dining room that flank it. Pendent lights illuminate the granite work surface and snack bar.

1 This dining room has more comfy armchairs than most, and it's used more too. The room is a family favorite for spreading out with the newspaper, doing homework, and chatting at the end of the day.

2 The master suite's entrance alcove with a window seat is a quiet place to relax with a book.

3 A door in the middle of the kitchen's appliance wall leads to a large pantry with floor-to-ceiling shelves and a planning desk. A lamp with a checked shade and a large framed print above the desk create an attractive focal point.

4 A room enveloped in wood has a warm ambience; whitewashing the wall's pine planks is a fresh touch that keeps it light and comfortable.

1

3,500 sq.ft. *Contemporary* Cabin

This traditional log home melds cabin style construction with today's must-have amenities: an attached garage, a first-floor master suite, and a great-room.

Taking its cue from frontier cabins, this Colorado log home uses square logs set in dovetail joints for the main walls, board-and-batten siding for the dormers, and cedar shingles for the peak of the cross gable. Corrugated steel roofing and a chimney and foundation faced with native river rock complete the look. Ten-foot-deep porches swathe the house on three sides, supported by ponderosa and lodgepole pine posts cut and peeled on-site. The rugged materials also give the house visual weight, grounding it to the wide-open Laramie Valley landscape that surrounds it.

Vintage log homes are often cramped and dark inside. But this modern interpretation combines log walls with the kind of timber-frame construction that's more common to cathedrals than cabins. The result is a large and lofty interior. The massive log trusses complement the hand-hewn appearance of the interior walls, and light-tone river rock gathered on-site climbs 20 feet up the gable-end wall to the roof peak.

Simple, clean finishes—slate tile floors, berber carpet, pine cabinetry, and steel accents and hardware—form a serene backdrop for the soaring architecture. Clerestory windows fill the interior with light. Groupings of comfortable, oversize furniture anchor the living spaces. Sparks of intense colors and patterns spring from a collection of Western and Native American art and artifacts, brightening a home that has timeless appeal.

1 Natural materials, traditional craftsmanship, and a weathered-looking roof give this contemporary log home vintage appeal.

2 A 20-foot-tall vaulted gable spans the spine of the house, soaring over the great-room, gallery, and master suite.

3 The kitchen's beaded-board pine cabinets blend with the warm honey-color logs. Glass cabinet fronts flank a polished-copper hood; black cookware complements the cabinet's simple, black-iron cabinet hardware. Marble countertops are acid-etched to add texture and minimize scratches.

4 The master bedroom combines a sitting area and a sleeping alcove anchored by a bed reminiscent of cross-bucked stable doors.

Rustic *Contemporary*

This house proves that you can wrap contemporary livability in a rustic structure that appears weather worn. The key is attention to detail: Instead of using galvanized sheeting for the roofing, for example, the architect chose corten—a steel alloy that is installed unfinished, quickly develops a thin protective coating of rust and, unlike regular steel, corrodes no further. The result mimics the attractive look of a decades-old, weather-beaten roof. Other rustic-looking examples in this home include irregularly sized logs with hand-cut dovetail joints and a hand-hewn interior finish (rather than uniform, machine-milled logs); a native, hand-selected river rock chimney (rather than faux-stone facing); and hand-cut-and-peeled ponderosa and lodgepole pine porch posts chosen for their unique, irregular appearance (rather than typical dimension-lumber supports). With care and research, you can achieve the same sense of authenticity with other styles as well.

3

2

4

1 Oversize, overstuffed lodge furnishings and Western and Native American themes complement the great-room's hand-hewn log walls and massive timber beams.

2 Across the passageway from the kitchen and tucked into the opposite corner of the great-room, the dining area is set off by a custom table fashioned from an oak wine cask and leather and wood chairs.

Main Level

PORCH

SITTING

MASTER BEDROOM

DINING

GALLERY

LIVING

CLOSET

BATH

ENTRY

KITCHEN

MECHANICAL

PORCH

GARAGE

Second Level

LOFT

OPEN TO KITCHEN, DINING/LIVING

BATH

BATH

GUEST BEDROOM

129

1

2

3

Good
Gothic

3,158 sq.ft.

F E A T U R E S

Detailing creates an attractive facade for this house, which was designed to fit comfortably on a narrow lot without skimping on interior space.

This home's slender facade, ornamental trim, and cozy porch invite you in from the street. The home suits its traditional neighborhood development, or TND, outside Indianapolis, but also offers advantages to other sites. For instance, many established subdivisions are faced with narrow leftover lots. This home could also blend into urban infill spaces where a newer style house might not fit in, stylistically or physically. Its farmhouse flavor makes it a natural in rural areas too.

Even if your site can handle the girth of a wider home, this plan has much to offer. On a standard size lot, for instance, you could move the house to one side rather than centering it on the property and use the

resulting open space for a large garden, tennis court, pool, or workshop.

Inside, the home feels anything but narrow. A spacious foyer welcomes guests and connects to a large dining room to one side and a stairway that leads to the upper level to the other.

The kitchen and family room flow together to create a space that belies the fact that the home is just 17 to 21 feet wide. These rooms span the entire width of the home, with windows on both sides allowing natural light and open views to stream through the interior.

Three bedrooms on the upper level, including the master suite, also make the most of the home's width.

Replacing the tunnel-like hallway often found in vintage Gothic homes, this contemporary version features a landing—at the top of the stairs—with doorways to the bedrooms and central bath.

The master suite consists of a bedroom, lounge, bathroom, and closet with generous room for dressing and storage. An intimate balcony is just right for relaxing under the stars before bed or surveying the morning weather.

The rear of the house holds one more concession to modern life: an attached two-car garage. This position is ideal because it remains secondary to the home's streetside presentation, allowing the house to shine.

Second Level   Main Level

4

5

Cast Your Lot If the home plan of your choice doesn't seem to be a good fit for your lot, don't rule it out right away. Some home plans can be adapted to suit the needs of a particular site. For example, here are three options for modifying this plan:

Bring a driveway in from the front. Although this home was designed to be "alley loaded," it can work in a "front loaded" lot by bringing a driveway the length of the lot. (You would need a deep lot, though, to accommodate the drive.)

Move garage doors from back to right. With this option, the drive could enter from the side on a corner lot or along the right side of the house from the front.

Detach the garage. The ridge of the garage roof runs side to side, while the home's main gable runs from front to back, which visually separates the garage from the house. Removing the garage entirely will not detract from the home's look. This option offers the opportunity to make a few more architectural changes. You could, for instance, add a window in the first floor laundry room above the space for the washer and dryer and yet another in the back wall of the master closet on the upper level. If you wanted to extend the back wall of the home a bit farther, you could add a staircase from the laundry to the master suite.

1 *This home's design makes the most of a narrow lot. The cross-gable wing adds space and visual interest, while a cozy porch offers shelter and old-fashioned sociability.*

2 *Authentic details abound in this Gothic Revival home, including the wood-planked porch, hood mold window trim, and entry door surrounded by sidelights and a transom.*

3 *This home offers three outdoor recreation areas, including this side porch that offers views of the backyard.*

4 *As seen from the dining room, the stairway appears attractive, not overemphasized. The door at left opens to a half bath. The door at right leads to the basement.*

5 *Tall windows and Victorian-style furnishings give this front parlor a refined, formal air.*

1 Built-in bookcases frame the family room's classically styled fireplace. Hardwood floors and wicker furnishings complement the period embellishments.

2 A compact kitchen adjoins the family room. The island serves for food preparation, conversation, and eating.

3 The master bedroom comprises half the upper level's square footage. In addition to the sleeping area, the suite features a bath with whirlpool tub, master closet, and dressing area.

4 The balcony off the master suite is a retreat within a retreat.

Carpenter *Gothic*

Another fanciful sub-style of the Victorian era, Carpenter Gothic houses are found in small towns and rural areas throughout the country. Although the style makes reference to some of the grandest buildings of all time—the elaborate Gothic cathedrals built in Europe during the Middle Ages—the execution is attractively modest, usually amounting to some ornamental modification of a plain, gable-front, two-story house. The style was given its name because just about any carpenter with a pattern book and scroll saw could execute the detailing—gothic-arched windows, gable-peak ornaments, and rake-board gingerbread. Inspired by Iowa artist Grant Wood's famous painting of a farmer and his daughter in front of their Carpenter Gothic farmhouse, the style has since become an icon for rural America.

3,211 sq.ft.

This home has no front or back advantage. Inspired by homes on Nantucket, it boasts great looks and views on both sides.

Watching the sun rise and set is easy to do in this home. Plenty of windows on the east and west sides make the rising sun hard to miss. Light streams through the house via the foyer's first floor eyebrow window and second-story clerestory windows.

This home is in Seattle, but its gabled, shingle-style exterior and interior detail is inspired by cottages far across the country on both Nantucket and Martha's Vineyard in Massachusetts. Woodwork and stonework add rich detail in the form of exposed ceiling beams, beaded board, artful balusters, and the stone hearth. With easy-care hardwood floors, living spaces that open to one another, and gathering places out front or back, this home presents a relaxed, open-arms ambience. Both of the home's "arms," an office and garage, stretch toward the street. The garage side reaches a bit longer, adding dimension to the home's footprint. An arbor and rose planters to either side help soften its welcome.

Paint & *Stain*

The kitchen, living, and dining rooms boast warm, buttery yellow walls. The ceiling paint is the same hue two shades deeper for more contrast with the white-painted beams. To ease the transition from kitchen to adjacent living spaces, the kitchen island is stained to match the dining and living room furniture rather than painted to match the kitchen cabinets.

All-Around
Beauty

1 *Some of the living room ceiling's boxed beams are purely decorative; some conceal structural supports. The mantel on the river-rock fireplace is an old beam salvaged from a warehouse. To the side of the fireplace, a television and sound system tuck into a built-in entertainment/display center. Mounted flush with the wall, speakers are barely visible.*

2 *A street-side courtyard of exposed aggregate and brushed concrete functions much like a porch. Over the entry, a glass canopy offers protection from the weather. Boxwood and perennials fill the planters; young roses will eventually climb the garage arbor.*

3 *The foyer features windows that reach nearly 25 feet high. Buttery walls and natural wood warm any intense surges of light.*

Main Level

Second Level

2

5

1 A massive island of granite-topped beaded-board accommodates a range, prep sink, seating, and storage. Just beyond, glass shelves stretch across a window for a sparkling display of houseplants and glassware.

2 With its own walk-in closet and full bath, the first floor office could become a master suite if needed. A utility hall—with pantry, bathroom, and laundry—smartly sits between the kitchen and attached garage.

3 Originally designed as a closet, this under-stair space in the kitchen now serves as an office. A second, more traditional office is located off the home's entry.

4 The raised built-in headboard provides privacy in the light-filled master bedroom.

5 Just outside the kitchen, a patio/porch spans the width of the house, ready to accommodate large gatherings. Porch supports are built of river rock, and the same exposed aggregate and brushed concrete used in the front courtyard forms the back patio.

6 A curve in the upstairs landing made this small library possible.

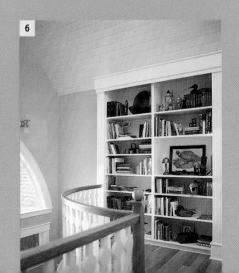

6

137

Wide Open Cozy

2,585 sq.ft.

Built on a wedge of property in an older neighborhood, this house balances an Arts and Crafts exterior by blending open, flowing and snug spaces inside.

The geometric lines of Arts and Crafts style strike a balance between the warmth of a traditional aesthetic and the open, clean feel of a contemporary look. This house reflects that idea, featuring contemporary interior elements wrapped in an exterior that melds into a mature neighborhood of Craftsman homes. The main level is wide open, with kitchen, living, dining, and conversation spaces open to one another. Tall ceilings and plenty of windows further expand the space. Furniture groupings, columns, and a jogged wall define the spaces without interrupting the flow.

Designed for frequent parties, this home is no stranger to gatherings of 10 or 100. The kitchen's island is the heart of the home and where every party begins. Small groups gathering for dinner often travel no farther than the island or the sitting area to the side of it; groups of people at the larger gatherings congregate in the dining and living spaces and on the pergola-topped patio outdoors.

As roomy as the lower level may be, decorative details yield a warm, intimate ambience. Trim finished in both white paint and stained wood, hardwood floors, and richly hued walls keep the spaces from feeling cold and sterile. While wide-open spaces prevail on the first floor, the home's upper level is a cozy and compartmentalized suite of bedrooms, bathrooms, and a laundry. The master suite sits directly over the living room, making it possible for both rooms to enjoy a fireplace off a shared chimney.

Light *Schemes*

Primary spaces in this home are lit by six to nine 75-watt halogen downlights that easily adjust for mood and ambience. Artwork in each room is highlighted with gallery-style dropped track lights. For a finishing touch, blown-glass pendent lights hang over the kitchen island and the table for soft, diffused lighting. Each type of lighting for each room is wired to its own control for the ultimate in lighting flexibility.

1 An exterior wrap of cedar shakes and lap siding blends this new house into its mature Arts and Crafts-style neighborhood. Any hint of contemporary style remains indoors.

2 Detail-and-repeat is a tried and true design strategy: At this home's entry, stone piers support both the square porch columns and a pair of lanterns that flank the entry path.

3 Downlights are tucked into the pergola's rafters to light the patio when the sun sets. Translucent roof panels and gas heaters make the space usable even on rainy or chilly days.

4 Despite its 12-foot ceilings and open floor plan, the living room feels cozy with its deep-hued walls, muntined transom windows, and an Arts and Crafts-style fireplace.

Main Level

Second Level

1 A kidney-shape island is the center of every gathering, no matter how large or small. The island is situated 18 inches farther from the wall cabinets than design standards dictate to make room for mingling and meal prep.

2 The office's entry-side location means that clients visiting the self-employed homeowner needn't traipse through the house to do business. Pocket doors fitted with shoji inserts block work from view when the day is done.

3 In the master bath, a beaded-board tub surround complements the geometry of the contemporary shower's stair-stepped glass walls.

4 Floor-to-ceiling window walls and doors blur the boundaries between indoors and out. Open the doors and the courtyard space becomes yet another room to enjoy.

141

Elegant
Cottage

2,963 sq.ft.

It looks like a woodland cottage. Step inside and you'll find an open, elegant one-level home that's designed for views, visitors, gatherings, and most of all, privacy.

If you have ever hosted overnight guests, you're familiar with the lack of privacy and traffic jams that can occur in a home when everyone's preparing for the day. This house solves those issues with an ingenious arrangement. One side of the home consists of a master suite and adjacent den for the homeowners. On the other side, two bedrooms (each with a full bath) serve children and friends who are frequent visitors. Separating the two sides are the living and dining rooms, kitchen and breakfast nook, screen porch, and family room. Guests can get up and start their day on their own without disrupting the homeowners—or vice versa. Public rooms are generously sized so everyone has plenty of personal space.

On the outside, the low-slung, one-story profile of this lap-sided house is intentionally modest. The goal? Classic appeal that doesn't necessarily reveal the elegant personality of the interior. Step inside the front door and the home reveals some big surprises: its spacious size, high vaulted ceilings, and a set of floor-to-ceiling windows that show off an amazing woodland view.

4   5

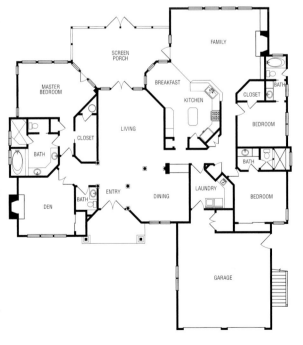

Main Level

Second Level

1 A broad hipped roof and cedar front and garage doors give this home a timeless cottage-like flair. Vines clambering over the garage arbor make a pleasant visual greeting.

2 This home is built on a slab on the highest point of a creekside property. A multitude of windows makes the most of woodland views.

3 The combination of detailed—but not fussy—millwork and casual honey-stained pine creates an elegant, casual look in the den. Cocoa-hued walls complement the pine with sophistication.

4 The family room is a perfect example of the home's relaxed formality. Classic furnishings seem at ease in the company of pine built-ins and pools of window light.

5 The simple kitchen's slate floor and stonelike countertops continue the home's color palette of honey, cocoa, and cream. A raised snack counter connects the kitchen to the family room.

1 The dining room with cathedral ceiling lies just inside the entry—a surprise given the home's facade. Two pillars separate the dining and living rooms.

2 Accessible from the master suite and both living and family rooms, the screen porch sees a lot of action during family gatherings. In this wooded location, the porch is as close as you can get to the out-doors without dealing with mosquitoes.

3 Nestled off the kitchen, between the liv-ing and family rooms, the breakfast nook is a quiet corner looking onto the screen porch.

4 Wide-slat shutters are a clean-lined means of gaining privacy in the master bed-room, which also opens onto the screen porch.

5 The home's pine theme continues in the master bath cabinets. Pine cabinetry is lower maintenance than painted wood because fingerprints and smudges are less apparent.

4

5

Baths for *Guests*

The owners of this South Carolina house have frequent overnight guests, so they included a full bath for each bedroom in their home. Although this approach boosts privacy and can speed morning prep time for your household, it also adds to construction, maintenance, and housekeeping costs. If you anticipate frequent company, consider these tips and alternatives in designing guest baths.

Design for two or more users. Place the tub or shower in one compartment and the vanity, with one or two sinks, in another.

Use a Jack-and-Jill plan. Two bedrooms share a bath between them.

Try a Hollywood bath. Two separate vanity rooms sit on either side of a main bath.

Go for three-quarters. If a full guest bath is prohibitive, a bath with sink, stool, and a shower can provide essential conveniences in a compact area.

Plan on It: The Family Studio

If the mudroom was the must-have room of the previous decade, the family studio is the top contender for the next. It's a hot idea that's 100-percent packed with practicality. A family studio is a utility room in which more than one person can do homework, work on school, art, or crafts projects, or pay bills and use the computer. You can pack a family studio into as little as a 10×10-foot space to serve a family of five. One homeowner describes the space as central to the hands-on aspect of her family's lives. A family studio definitely helps keep the peace. It eliminates competition for kitchen counter and table space and quashes the need to hustle someone through a project so a room can be tidied.

Ideally a family studio is located behind a closed door. That's key: It provides space in which you can leave in-progress projects out for completion. It's also best to locate a family studio just off the kitchen, where adults working on meals can answer children's questions and offer help without running through the house (that is, unless the adults aren't already in the studio working on their own things!). For those who want their children to use the computer in a central supervised location, family studios are an excellent option.

You can design a family studio to incorporate a mudroom, laundry, potting center, and home office, or it can be the last in a succession of these rooms. Some plans locate the family studio just off the kitchen en route to the family's laundry/mudroom/locker room. By the time family arrives at the kitchen, packs, gear, and dirty duds are in their proper places.

1

Elements of a Family Studio

Use these tips to create a family studio that suits the needs of your family:

Plan work surfaces, allowing at least a 30- to 36-inch stretch for each person who will regularly use the space. Tables, peninsulas, and islands come in handy for joint efforts. A blend of seated and standing height counters is also wise.

Allow computer hookups for several terminals, at least two, with surface on either side for spreading out. Network the computers to share a printer and other peripherals.

Think public and private. Everyone will use the studio, but each needs a storage space to call his or her own.

Prepare for a mess by using wipe-clean surfaces. This is the place where laminate countertops and vinyl floors reign.

Add a sink for fast cleanup of arts and craft projects.

Give it good looks. This utility room is also a family gathering place. Choose colors you like and hang corkboard to display artwork, notes, and photos.

Light it up with a combination of natural, general, and task lighting. If the view in or out isn't great, use glass-block windows.

Think big and make your workroom as roomy as you possibly can. You'll be surprised at how much your family will use the space.

1 Siblings can snack, work on a project, or tackle a game at this studio's peninsula. A painting and corkboard full of family snapshots add personality and warmth.

2 This studio includes a locker for each family member, fitted with hooks and adjustable laminate shelves.

3 Daylight filters into the studio through the generous glass-block interior windows and the etched glass door. Broad, flat drawers at the desk are ideal for storing oversize artwork; the chair casters make it easy to roll to another surface.

Ceiling Treatments

Ceiling detail adds substantial character, drama, and value to a home. It can visually raise, lower, or angle a ceiling—or expose and embellish its surface or structure.

You can carry out simple ceiling treatments, such as covering the surface with beaded board, through an entire level or home. More elaborate treatments, such as exposed beams, are best limited to feature spaces such as kitchens, gathering areas, or dining rooms. As you browse the treatments shown here and throughout the book, consider how you can use ceiling style strategically. **Vaults, beams,** and **exposed structures** add volume to a room, making the space feel larger than it actually is. **Changes in ceiling height or type** help define rooms in open, wall-free areas. For texture, you can **detail flat ceilings** with paint, wallpaper, beaded board and other paneling, embossed metal, and moldings.

1 Clerestory windows bring light and treetop views to this vaulted, beam-ceiling room. These ceilings are dressed with paneling; drywall works as well.

2 Beautifully detailed trusses stretch across the vaulted ceiling of this first floor room and frame the views from the stairway landing. The white trusses are accented with mahogany to complement the railings.

3 Spokes of painted and natural-finish wood slats circle a central skylight to create a gazebolike feel in this dining area.

4 Embossed metal is set into a tray ceiling that's framed with painted drywall and a band of hardwood trim. The result is an old-world look. As an alternative, you can paint embossed wallpaper to resemble tin, copper, or tooled leather.

5 A dropped ceiling within this home's vaulted open space cozies up the kitchen.

6 By taking the ceiling paint color 18 inches down the living room walls, the ceiling appears higher, and the room appears larger.

Garages

The automobiles that made suburbia possible have created an architectural nightmare: domineering garages. Some call them "snout houses," and not always with affection! The problem is, these massive drive-in shelters can push back the more charming portions of a house, making it appear unwelcoming and faceless. Like any conundrum, you have options—options that make you wonder why builders and architects didn't suggest them in the first place. (Many of the case studies in this book display creative garage solutions, so check them out.)

For alternatives to the big-box-out-front, try these ideas for attractively melding your car shelter into your home.

Alter the roofline or walls. For a multicar garage, drop the roofline or set back the footprint of one or more stalls.

Build a side entry. Corner lots often allow drives and garage entry from the side rather than front of the house. You can outfit the streetside wall with attractive windows to complement the house.

Go for an angle. This is a less severe variation on the side entry. Sometimes you can angle your garage a few degrees for much improved presentation.

Let them walk. If you really don't *need* direct access to more than one vehicle, house others in a detached garage elsewhere on the property. If you're sheltering kids' cars, let them walk a few feet to get to their cars.

Lead the way. Incorporate flagstone, brick, or a different pattern in your drive to function as a walk, leading friends to your front door.

Get dressed! Give your garage more appeal—and a more human-scale welcome—with decorative touches: doors that complement the home's architectural style, individual lighting fixtures, planters between stalls, short trellises with vining plants over the doors, a nearby bench, or a porch that wraps around to a front door walk. Such elements are friendlier than standard closed garage doors.

1 Here's a big house with a better solution to the big garage out front: a big garage out back. The covered portico allows family or friends to hop in a car under shelter and use a side entry; the garage is attached to the back of the house.

2 Two windows with a door between make a one-story detached garage look like a guest house until you see the garage doors that face the alley. To gain benefits of an attached garage, a covered porch stretches to the home's main porch, offering a sheltered path from house to car.

3 Built at a right angle to the house it serves, this attached garage is as handsome as the home itself—without dominating it. The shelter features a roofline similar to the house, board-and-batten siding running vertically to the home's horizontal siding, shared color, detailed door surrounds, and individual light fixtures over each door.

4 A solid wall of garage doors that dominates a house can be unwelcoming to visitors and ultimately unattractive to future buyers. What would help? A short arbor over the length for vining or hanging plants, sconce lighting between doors, and a planter of bright flowers placed on the right to draw visitors toward the door.

151

5,408 sq.ft.

Cast in the cozy, unassuming style of a bungalow, this home offers both room enough for a growing family and one-level living when the nest empties. A well-designed lower level makes it all possible.

With just more than 5,400 square feet beneath its gabled roof, this unpretentious house is surprisingly accommodating. While many Craftsman-era bungalows would boost capacity by slipping bedrooms beneath the eaves in an upper half story, this home makes room below. A fully finished below-grade level includes five bedrooms, three baths, and a kitchenette—plus crafts, billiards, and recreation rooms that host family and friends. A window-well courtyard and two deep, broad landscaped window wells provide light and egress.

With no need for an upper half story over the main floor, first floor ceilings and windows follow the roof to its peak. Within the airy space, there's a family room, dining room, two-cook kitchen, and breakfast room. Private spaces—the homeowners' office and master bedroom suite—claim one side of the first floor. Family and friends can gather on the home's broad front porch or head inside through the family room to the kitchen area, which is supported by a screen porch off the breakfast room. A smart suite of rooms that cater to active family life tucks between the kitchen and the garage. It includes a laundry/mudroom, half bath, large pantry, and small office where kids can do homework and surf the Internet supervised by their nearby parents.

Big-Boned Bungalow

1

1 This home's gray and white color scheme and natural materials recall Craftsman-era architecture. Its gabled roof and one-story proportions belie the size of the house.

2 Glass-front, built-in bookshelves flank the family room hearth; the door details echo the home's window styling. Windows above the broad mantel brighten the room and afford views of the trees.

3 Divided-light windows surround a vintage-look front door. The welcoming foyer separates private rooms from public spaces on the main floor.

4 Retrofit for sink service, a copper tub adds soft luster to the simple, pretty laundry/mudroom.

153

1 2

3

1 *Trusses that support the vaulted ceiling make the large two-cook kitchen feel open and cozy.*

2 *Roomy banquette seating in the breakfast room is ideal for conversation or games as well as casual dining.*

3 *Stretching from one side of the dining room to the other, the built-in sideboard looks like an antique. Overhead, a coffered ceiling is finished with trim, creating an unpretentious detail.*

4 *A transom window above the master bathtub beautifies this cozy retreat.*

5 *Chimneys anchor both sides of the home, with fireplaces in the family room and master bedroom.*

Main Level

Second Level

155

5,326 sq.ft.

Although it looks as if it has been added onto over several generations of homeowners, this luxurious, rambling home is brand new. Inside, it incorporates both formal and casually styled living spaces with grace and refinement.

This Georgia house is built in the tradition of many Southern homes, featuring front porches for kicking back with sweet tea and a two-story body, with wings on either side. Nevertheless, the house is freshly built and designed for modern living.

The interior features a one-level living option, with rooms arranged so heat and air-conditioning can be closed off from upper and terrace levels when the entire family isn't home. An entry separates private spaces (a study, master suite, and guest suite)—an ideal setup for a couple with an infant. The great-room, dining room, and staircase also form a buffer between public rooms and the private spaces. The latter, the kitchen, breakfast room, and keeping room, all open onto a screen porch and deck. A home office opens onto a front porch, and a laundry and large pantry conveniently slip between kitchen and garage. Bedrooms and baths for older children, along with a large media room, are on the second level. The floor plan is ideal for an active family that likes to entertain. For example, when the kids gather with friends in the keeping room, adults can take over the great-room, screen porch, or study.

Southern
Hospitality

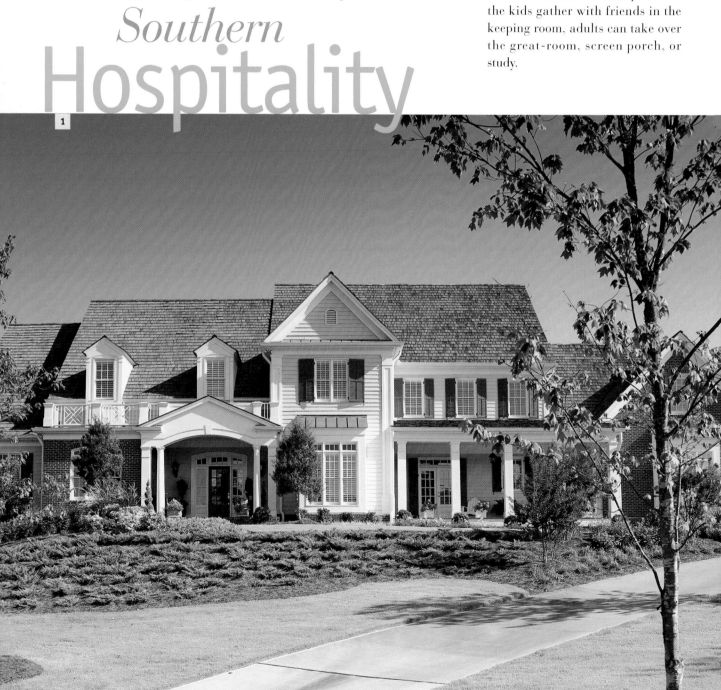

Design *Details*

The homeowners found this home as it was being built. They purchased it and were able to work with the builders on the details. They added an interior designer to the professional team and upgraded surface materials, lighting fixtures (adding feature fixtures and recessed lighting), and also beefed up the architectural moldings, trim, and built-in furnishings. The whole team collaborated on windows and ceiling treatments to create themes for particular spaces. In the great-room and keeping room, for instance, ceilings rise to a plane rather than a peak for volume that's cozy rather than awe-inspiring. The great-room features elegant Palladian windows and a smooth finish ceiling surface. The keeping room features a paneled-and-beamed ceiling and quarter-round windows on either side of the hearth for a rustic look.

2

3

1 *Roomy porches, shutters, dormer windows, and a roof balustrade embrace this house in Southern-style tradition. A simple exterior of brick and lap siding is topped with a textural cedar shake roof.*

2 *Open to the family room and its windows of light, the kitchen's dark features—richly stained cabinets and granite countertops—appear handsome, not oppressive.*

3 *Traditional wainscoting and a rich wall color create an elegant formal dining room. After a meal, guests can move onto one of the front porches through the French doors.*

4 *Olive-stained built-ins, trim, and shuttered windows give the study an English pub look.*

4

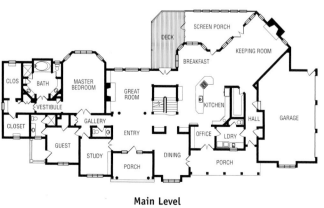

Main Level

Upper Level

1 The home's great-room is sized for intimate entertaining. The Palladian window and classic moldings lend a formal, dignified air.

2 A tray ceiling rimmed with down-lighting, soft taupe walls, and velvet draperies establish the master bedroom's luxe look.

3 A wood vanity and matching chair resemble elegant furniture in the master bath. Limestone surfaces the floor and countertop.

4 A stacked-stone hearth, tongue-and-groove paneling, and white ceiling beams give the keeping room plenty of texture. The shape of the quarter-round windows is echoed in the armoire detailing, a nice touch.

5 The home's exterior view intrigues onlookers with an angled screen porch, diagonally placed chimney, and sun-catching feature windows.

Family-Friendly Habitat

4,471 sq.ft.

A family home rimmed with porches, patios, and decks stretches high and wide—not deep—on a broad, shallow lot.

This home may be large, but the allure of its exterior details and blend of natural materials and warm interior colors make it a welcoming place that's not at all intimidating.

A broad front covered porch with sets of double doors greet guests. Adjacent to the porch, the long wall of the three-car garage extends like an arm calling you to come on in. The far set of doors opens to the master suite area; the near set opens to the home's slate-floored foyer. Inside, the two-story space immediately presents an open floor plan with great-room windows that feature grand views out back.

To the right of the entry, the master wing includes a sitting room, bedroom, bath, and walk-in closet. The sitting area has its own entrance to the front porch, and the bedroom opens to a private back deck. One-level living is an option here. The grandly scaled two-story great-room, just a few steps in from the foyer, is the main level's centerpiece. Thick, dark ceiling beams, a rugged wood mantel, and log storage beneath the hearth create a lodgelike ambience.

The kitchen is a more private affair, set away from the entry view and accessible via a door between the great-room and dining room. The L-shape kitchen features an island and a brick divider and opens onto a hearth room and breakfast/sunroom to make sheltered, intimate family spaces.

In enclosed rooms parallel to the family spaces, the laundry room, mudroom, powder room, a door to the garage, and a back staircase that leads upstairs to the children's bedrooms are located. The bedrooms are also accessible from the foyer staircase and bridge. Upstairs, a Jack-and-Jill-style bath/closet arrangement serves two of the sleeping rooms; another room has its own full bath and closet. A garage-topping bonus room houses a home business, and an adjacent hallway nook just beyond is furnished as an L-shape computer workstation. By linking the children's bedrooms to the garage entry, mudroom, and laundry, it's easy for the kids to stay organized (and clean) as they head in and out of the house with backpacks, coats, hats, and gear.

Below grade, the basement is finished with entertaining in mind: Media and billiards rooms and a wet bar cover all the bases.

Where covered porches welcome streetside guests at the front door and off the driveway, screen porches and decks to the side and back of the home offer plenty of opportunity to watch birds that live in the woods.

1 Broad, gentle arches at the window tops and porch fascias soften the steep peaks of the roofline. One set of double doors on the front porch leads to the foyer; the other set leads to the master suite.

2 A wall of windows and French doors unites the outdoors with the great-room. The stone hearth, wood floors, and leather sofas enhance the natural aspects of the home.

3 The bold wall colors—sunny yellow for the entry and rich red for spaces above and to the sides—create interest and depth and keep the high ceiling from feeling imposing.

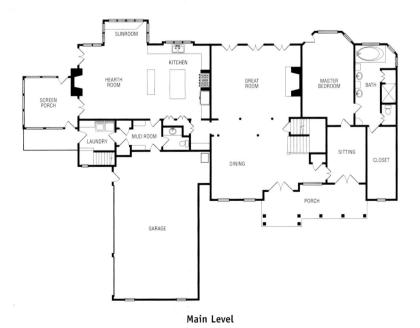

Main Level

Upper Level

1 A wood-topped brick island visually divides the kitchen from the adjacent hearth room and offers a safe, easy-to-reach site for the microwave oven.

2 A cozy hearth room and breakfast/sun-room are open to the kitchen. On the other side of the kitchen is a larger, more formal great-room.

3 The master bedroom's cool green walls and blue bedding and rugs are a soothing complement to the warm pine floors.

4 The shapely legs of a console sink, hexagonal tiles on the floor, and candle-style sconces create an air of old-fashioned ambience in the master bath.

5 The foyer and great-room open to the second floor, so family members on different levels feel connected. The upstairs bridge leads to children's bedrooms.

Modern Day Arts and Crafts

4,236 sq.ft.

Exceptionally rich in architectural details but light in spirit, this Michigan home has an Arts and Crafts-inspired facade—and offers generous living space in what appears to be a one-story house.

How do you blend a love for the architectural richness and woodwork of Arts and Crafts-era houses with a penchant for light, airy modern-day style? You carefully embrace some Arts and Crafts themes and bypass others. The exterior of this house, for example, features porch pillars that taper into river rock posts, a big front porch, classic sash windows, shutters, and window boxes. But you won't find heavy Craftsman-era details such as deep overhangs and exposed rafters.

To achieve Craftsman flavor without the extra weight that comes with a house full of stained woodwork, most of the woodwork in this house is painted. Some select pieces of woodwork—the front door, newel posts, and portions of the fireplace surround—are stained. The goal was a family home that's rich in detail yet light and bright. Woodwork for this home was crafted on-site or in the builder's shop.

Trim details and motif themes are repeated throughout this home, a technique that boosts the details' impact. For example, the same wainscoting style appears in the dining room and around the tub in the master bath. The dining room's banded door style hutch also is used in kitchen cupboard doors. And the cozy alcove and bracket trim that surrounds the living room fireplace is found yet again in the niche surrounding the master bath. Furthermore, the paneling for the mudroom lockers features the same style that's on the living room ceiling. Square tile and color also carry through the first level.

From a floor plan perspective, this grand-size home offers plenty of living space without looking massive because it's nestled into a slope. To passersby, it looks like a roomy one-story structure. The main level includes a spacious living room, dining room, den, kitchen, mudroom, laundry, and master suite. Secondary bedrooms and a family room with kitchenette are located on the fully finished walk-out basement level. The distinct levels offer an advantageous budget opportunity as well. The lower level can be as richly detailed as the main level, or it can be done more simply.

1 By pressing this house into the top of a gentle slope, it looks like a one-story bungalow. Its fully finished second walk-out level is out of view.

2 The L-shape mudroom hugs the laundry and has entries linking it to the back porch and garage. Bin storage beneath the window seat and lockers holds seasonal outerwear and bulky gear.

3 Lightening the Arts and Crafts-era tradition of all stained wood, this house features creamy white painted trim with just some pieces stained. Here, the classic Craftsman-style front door and newel posts are stained.

4 A stained glass Arts and Crafts-style pendent fixture over the table is a focal point in the dining room.

5 A truncated pillar stands on a white built-in bookcase beside the front door, defining the foyer and den spaces. It makes a comfy reading nook too.

Theme *Scheme*

A single element that you love can ignite decorating themes for an entire house. The color palette for this home came from the tile fireplace surround: an Arts and Crafts blend of squares in flecked greens, gray-blue, coppery red, and brilliant gold. Working from the tile, an interior designer chose several shades of green from a single paint strip for seamless flow. The lightest shade is used on living room walls, a medium hue for the kitchen, and the den gets the darkest version. The tile also inspired the dining room's deep brown-red walls and additional square tile designs, including the arrangement of tiles that dress the kitchen and master bath.

165

1 The dining room celebrates texture with brown-red walls and furnishings, creamy wainscoting, and a glass-fronted hutch. The Craftsman-style hanging fixture is like a piece of jewelry, adding sparkle and luster to the entire room.

2 An alcove around the fireplace lends simple detail to the family room. The cabinet design and wall trim above are in keeping with the home's wainscoting found in other rooms. Only the horizontal tops of the mantel and cabinets are left unpainted.

3 For a look that seems to have evolved over time, the kitchen features a mix of pieces: creamy cabinets, a painted hutch (not visible), and a cherry and granite island. Halogen pendents are a contemporary touch that's powerful but not obtrusive.

1

2

Main Level

Upper Level

Free Flowing Ranch

5,200 sq.ft.

A classic rambler with loads of wow-power underscores two points: A contemporary look can have spirit and warmth; and universal, barrier-free home design can be beautiful.

Homesites that slope gently into wooded areas are ideal for ranch-style houses that have light-filled, walk-out levels. This St. Louis home makes the most of its location with a two-story garden atrium that brings the outdoors in.

Light sparkling through the front door's transom and sidelights suggests the look that lies beyond. Step inside and you see the showstopping atrium. The dining room opens to the left; the great-room and kitchen, ahead and to the left. The master suite, with its own transoms and sidelights, also has atrium views.

Ceiling styles change to define main-level spaces. A vaulted, paneled ceiling rises over the great-room and kitchen. Painted beams over the breakfast area provide transition between the vaulted great-room and kitchen, and the dining room's lower ceiling enables intimate meals.

While the atrium sets a contemporary attitude for this house, it's just the first of the home's distinctions. Although the architectural style is spacious, clean, and contemporary, the house is furnished and detailed with a rugged stone fireplace, paneled ceilings, painted beams, and beaded-board wainscoting. Carefully selected fabrics infuse country spirit and warmth for an overall, feel-good mix. The home also features another layer of distinction, but it's one you won't see immediately: The house incorporates universal, barrier-free design principles, so it will always be comfortable for its owners and their guests.

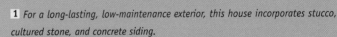

1 For a long-lasting, low-maintenance exterior, this house incorporates stucco, cultured stone, and concrete siding.

2 The first floor study is planned for simple conversion to a barrier-free bedroom. It's attached to a fully barrier-free bathroom and adjacent to the elevator.

3 A skylight and a mass of recessed cans light the kitchen and its boomerang-shape island. Plenty of maneuvering space is allowed for someone in a wheelchair or a kitchen full of guests.

4 A partial wall separates the dining and living rooms but allows views of the atrium and backyard. The ceiling here is coffered for intimacy.

5 This house has contemporary structure, but the breakfast area's beaded-board wainscoting, furnishings, and painted beams infuse country spirit.

1

4

2

3

Universal Barrier-Free Design

A house that's designed with universal or barrier-free design principles in mind is a home that's comfortable, whether you're a child or an adult, if you strain your back playing ball over the weekend, or if you use a wheelchair.

In this home, universal ideas start at the front door. It's a step-free stroll from street level through the garage to the mudroom. The tall garage makes room for a van and ramp access to the mudroom. On the main level, the study/bedroom space and adjoining bath and closet are totally barrier-free. Temperature and light controls and a panic button that can flash exterior lights and raise the garage doors for emergency personnel are located at bedside. An elevator accesses the home's lower level, and the path to the family room and patio is bump-free. The home has several safe exits for wheelchairs. The handful of design strategies that follow outline a crash course in universal barrier-free design moves. Try incorporating as many elements as possible.

Know the comfortable reach range. Locate door handles, appliances, electrical switches, and outlets 15 to 48 inches from the floor.

Make space. Minimum wheelchair passage is 32 inches, but consider planning for 48 inches. This much room makes moving furniture a breeze too. Allow for 60-inch turning radius and plenty of approach space in front of appliances, closets, and countertops.

Eliminate bumps. Add curb-free doorway thresholds, level flooring surface changes, and curb-free showers for roll-in access. Choose solid, bump-free flooring or carpet.

Add ease and comforts. Choose lever-style door handles, sink basins and counters no higher than 34 inches, and knee clearance 27 inches high, 30 inches wide, and 19 inches deep. Go with scaldproof thermostatically controlled or pressure-balanced water valves. Add grab bars at the toilet, bath, and shower seat. Position the toilet seat 17–19 inches from the floor. Shallow vanities or side-mounted faucets allow for easy reach access. Choose mirrors angled or sized with a lower edge no more than 40 inches from the floor.

For more information on universal design, contact www.aarp.org/universalhome.

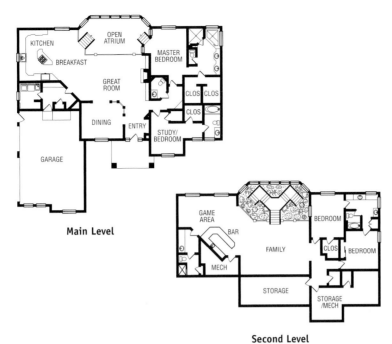

Main Level

Second Level

1 The master bath includes a sitting ledge at the tub, a built-in dressing table, and a threshold-free shower (not in view) for easy roll-in access if homeowners need barrier-free elements.

2 In the fully barrier-free bathroom, the sink vanity is open for roll-up or seated access. Plumbing is encased to avoid getting burned by hot pipes, yet there's room for knees and toes. An angled vanity mirror and grab bars near the toilet round out the features.

3 This wheelchair-accessible closet makes full use of wall space with low-mounted drawers and pull-down racks. An air-hydraulic system operates the pull-down racks, which pull down with a bar and slowly retract upward on their own.

4 The master suite, which opens onto the atrium, has transom-topped doors and sidelights that capture views of the woods.

5 An open staircase of stained and painted wood and see-through panels makes the most of atrium views. The landing serves as a year-round indoor garden.

6 An elevator, helpful to those on crutches or requiring a wheelchair, requires no more than a 4×5-foot space on both levels. That's enough to ferry two people, one seated in a wheelchair, up and down the home's levels.

7 The view of the atrium is as impressive as the view from inside out. The interior stairway is visible through the two-story windows.

Wired for the Future

You may think that plumbing and wiring your home for media and computing have nothing in common. They do. Roughing in the plumbing for all potential sinks and bathrooms when your home is being built makes financial sense. And the same is true of wiring. If you're the wired type and enjoy multimedia and computing functions, laying wire during construction can save you a third to a fifth of the cost of retrofitting it later.

The Big Tip

Whether your interest is television, a home theater, a whole-house sound system that plants near-invisible speakers in every room of the house, a family computer network, or a total home automation system that enables you to see who's at the front door while you watch a movie in the basement, call a home automation professional for a consultation. Even if you don't build a "smart house," you'll learn about the latest technologies available for your home.

During your meeting, inquire about high-tech options and speed, ask what technologies are developing, and find out what's needed to support them and how quickly such technologies can become outdated.

For instance, wireless components that make family computer networks simpler to create outside a central computing room are now available. But don't expect wire to totally drop out of the scene.

TV Opportunity

Despite advances in technology, a pertinent home design question is where to put the TV set or sets. Browse the following options for inspired ideas.

And while you're at it, keep an open mind about flat-screen TVs,

which can be hung on the wall. Current prices for plasma and liquid crystal display screens seem high, but they can be a budget-wise choice

when you figure in the cost of purchasing an entertainment center or cabinetry to house standard television sets.

Wire Speak	Get comfy with some of this jargon if you're a wired type, you'll use it; and if you're not, it's more specific than saying "wires" or "thingy."

POTS. Plain Old Telephone Service wire. This old-style multistrand, four-wire "bell wire" in a plastic sheath works well for telephones and faxes, but not for high-speed data transmission.

Category 5 vs. Category 1. Cat-5 is high-quality wire for voice and data transmission. Cat-1 telephone wire is for POTS only and carries signals at less than 4 megabits per second. Cat-5, on the other hand, carries at 100 megabits per second; enhanced Cat-5e carries at 350.

Home Run or Star vs. Daisy Chain. A home-run wiring scheme runs a wire or cable from a centrally located distribution panel to a given outlet box. To visualize it, imagine that the panel is a ball diamond, outlet boxes are "out-of-the-park home runs." A daisy-chain wiring pattern runs a wire or cable from the panel to a series of outlets, similar to traditional plumbing or electrical service.

F-connectors. These screw-type connectors attach video cable such as RG59 or RG6 to televisions, VCRs, DVD players, and other video devices.

RG6 vs. RG59. RG6 is enhanced coaxial TV-video cable. It's better shielded than the RG59 cable that's installed in most homes now. Signal loss for RG6 is 5.9 decibels per hundred feet; for RG59 it's 7.1. And speed? POTS wire moves data as fast as hand-pumped water from a well; RG6 runs like an open fire hydrant.

RJ45 vs. RJ11. Standard connectors that plug a telephone set into a wall outlet are RJ11 plugs and jacks. They're plastic and have space for six conductors. That said, they usually have four conductors; some just two. RJ45 plugs and jacks, used in data installations, are larger than RJ11s with space for eight conductors, but six are usually present.

1 A television is cleverly concealed over a fireplace, behind a painting. For viewing, the painting slides up mounted hardware to reveal the TV. You can use this technique with a mirror in place of the painting.

2 A primitive-looking blanket chest at the foot of this bed holds a TV, not blankets and sweaters. A carpenter split the chest's lid and fitted a shelf with hardware to create a self-rising TV platform that tucks away when it's not in use.

3 Deep box TVs are slowly giving way to flat-screen technologies, reducing (though not eliminating) the need for deep TV cabinets. Most are beautifully designed, so there's little need to hide them. Likewise, with such screens becoming part of a home networking/computing/comfort control center, they're sure to be in constant use. This one is mounted on a wall cabinet; the surrounding cabinets hold TV-related supplies.

1

Home Theaters

The real estate value of that cave-like space in your basement has gone way up thanks to the popularity of home theaters. Home theaters need everything that a window-free, below-grade level has to offer: darkness, separation from household activity, and shape. Most basements are rectangular, and that's the shape audio-video experts recommend for rich, realistic sound. You will need to install rugs or carpet over that hard basement floor, though. Hard surfaces increase sound distortion; fabrics reduce it. Here's a crash course in home theater setup.

Relate screen size to your seating plan. Keep this in mind when you're thinking of that wall-size screen: For optimum viewing, home theater experts recommend a seating distance that's two to two-and-a-half times the width of a screen. For example, chairs should be 54 to 68 inches from a 27-inch-wide screen.

Front-projection systems replicate the experience of sitting in a movie theater but depend on complete darkness. Rear-projection systems and picture-tube TVs produce a picture that looks as good with lights on as off. If entertaining figures into your media mix, go with the latter.

Create full surround-sound with five speakers. Place one speaker on each side of the TV screen, level with your ears when you're seated and about 3 feet away from side walls. Plant two behind the sofa about 6 to 8 feet off the floor and at least as wide apart as the front pair. Place the fifth one on top of the TV to distribute the dialogue. If you're an action-movie buff, you'll enjoy a sub-woofer that intensifies the soundtrack's bass. Put it beneath the screen.

Store equipment in a well-ventilated cabinet or closet.

Go with dimmer light switches over toggle style for light control.

Get help from a pro who is well-versed in the latest technologies and gadgetry. Consult a local home theater specialist: Look in the phone directory under "Home Theater" or "Audio/Video."

1 A direct-vent, gas-fueled fireplace does not require a chimney above and, therefore, creates the perfect niche for a TV. Slide-away, bleached pine doors are part of the paneling and lighted display niches.

2 If a small TV is all you want, tuck one into cabinetry. This one swings into view on a swivel shelf.

3 Kitchens that open to living space may be able to tap this idea in which the TV backs into the kitchen island.

4 This lower-level home theater is finished with knotty white pine siding for a comfortable lodge look. The hollowed-out pine logs conceal structural steel posts. Speakers hide under the TV screen; they're tucked behind black grill cloth and a lumber frame. A rubber pad and commercial-grade carpeting cover the concrete slab. Foam pads may deteriorate in humid conditions.

After the planning for your project is under way, you'll soon find yourself at the moment of truth, when the dream house you envision and the reality of your budget meet. This chapter introduces you to ways to make that meeting a happy one, beginning with an example of a striking custom home that was built for about 40 percent less than most generic builder homes. The strategies to accomplish such a job are highlighted.

In this chapter you also discover situations in which it's smart to spend more money up front to give yourself a healthier, more livable, more efficient and flexible house—one that will accommodate your needs and those of your evolving family and lifestyle for years, or perhaps decades, to come. Planning will save you money in the long run and prevent you from having to sell your house prematurely—and thereby save you the big costs associated with buying, selling, and moving.

Along the way you'll find strategy after strategy for saving money on financing, taxes, materials, and labor. You'll even find ways to save on architect's and interior designer's services.

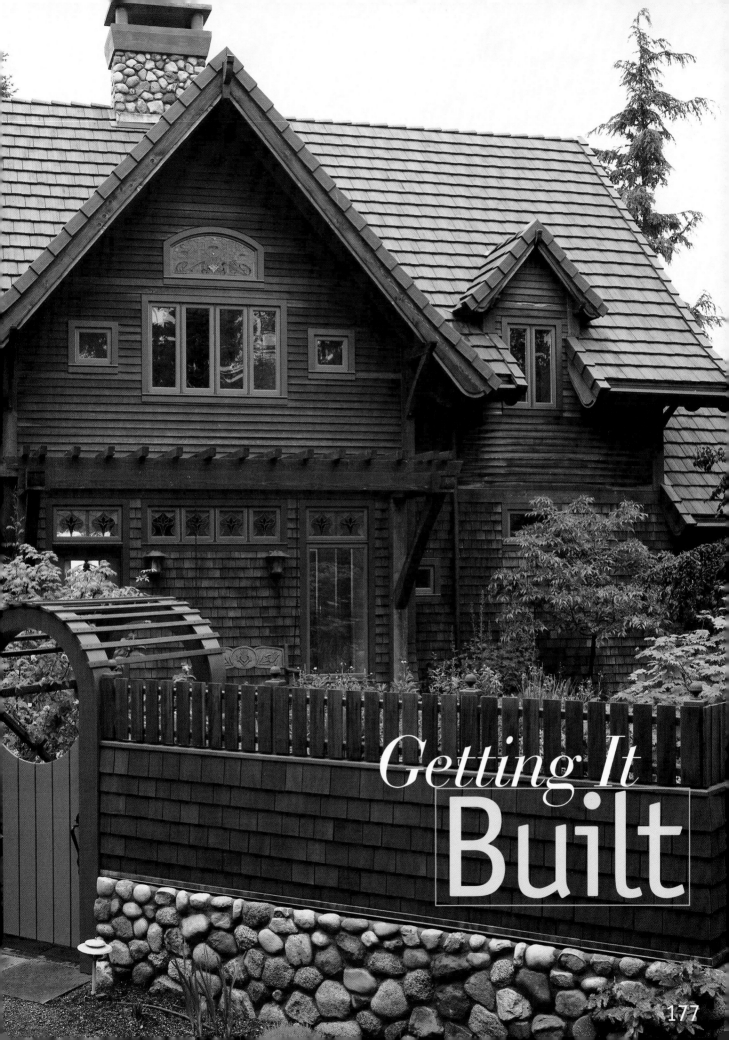

Getting It
Built

1

Building on a Budget

This welcoming, English country-style home cost nearly 40 percent less than the average new home built in its suburban Seattle neighborhood. Yet it has much more panache than a standard builder home, due in part to the following strategies that almost any home-owner can use.

Sketch your own floor plans. You can design the house yourself and use an architect only to make sure everything is up to code and to create the final blueprints. Making use of an architect in this way may cost as little as 1 percent of the construction costs, as opposed to the typical 10 to 15 percent fee an architect charges for full-service design and construction supervision fee.

Build on a square foundation. A house built on a square foundation is least expensive to build, and it doesn't necessarily mean you have to live in a box. In this example, for instance, exterior walls angle to form bay windows on both floors. Other details include a round window, embellishments called quoins at the corners of the house, and dentil molding at the soffit where the roof meets the wall. Ten-and-a-half-foot ceilings in the living room and 9½-foot ceilings throughout the rest of the house add to the perception of space in the modest 1,880-square-foot home.

Negotiate with your contractor. Find a builder who's willing to let you perform some of the labor and provide certain supplies.

Be a good shopper. Negotiate directly with suppliers. This home features a jetted tub bought at 60 percent discount, and many other big-ticket items were obtained at similar savings. Thrift shops, garage sales, and used-furniture stores are sources of distinctive furnishings and accessories at rock-bottom prices.

Invest some sweat equity. Install your own molding and fireplace surrounds; caulk seams and fill nail holes. Performing these jobs can save you $3,000 to $4,000. Experts estimate that 85 percent of the cost of a paint job is labor, so picking up a brush and roller can add up to big savings on your behalf.

Use alternative materials. Depending on where you live, pine can cost as low as one-tenth as much as oak. In this house, substituting pine for flooring instead of the hardwood saved more than $10,000.

Salvage. Look for a home that someone is remodeling or tearing down. You may be able to buy light fixtures (many fixtures in this house were salvaged), plants, flagstones, and landscaping timbers for little outlay. Or check directories under "Building Materials—Used." Some carry vintage details that are no longer available new.

1 Built on a bargain-priced lot between the trees of an apple orchard, this home offers all the detail of more expensive houses, including all-vinyl windows, old-fashioned moldings, and a pediment entry with columns purchased from a lumberyard.

2 The homeowner built the cabinets from pine at a fraction of the cost of oak. The covered chair (a $14 office surplus find) is reupholstered in chintz.

3 Mature trees and aged flagstone grace the backyard. All were salvaged from nearby home-remodeling projects at a fraction of the items' retail values.

4 The homeowners installed the stock fireplace surround themselves, as well as all the interior molding, for a substantial savings on labor cost. A glazed paint finish in two shades of pink gives this room flair at a fraction of the cost of premium wallcovering.

5 Interior detailing is similarly striking: Elegant white-painted columns (a surprisingly inexpensive stock item) flank the passage between the dramatic entry and the living room a few steps down. Mellow pine floors begin here and continue throughout the first floor. The large rug, a museum-quality find, cost only $50 at a garage sale.

179

Plan Smart to Cut Costs

If you don't feel up to drawing your own floor plan, or if you've already found a plan you like, don't worry. You can still save money. Almost any floor plan can be modified to include cost-saving features. Here are a few common money-saving choices.

Standard window and door sizes. Select door sizes such as exterior doors that are 3'×8'6" high and interior doors that are 2'8"×6'8" inches high. Windows come in a variety of standard sizes. Want bigger doors and windows? Create the shape you want by combining conventional sizes.

Conventional lumber lengths. Design walls and floors so standard lumber lengths can be used, resulting in less material waste and less labor cost. Use minimal special order beams.

Simple roof design. Conventional rooflines, with common 10:12 or 12:12 pitches, are simple to frame and can often be constructed of money-saving prefabricated trusses. More complicated rooflines with several hips, gables, and steep pitches add expense because they require more skill and time to frame. A truss manufacturer can't prefabricate such rooflines.

Minimal columns and beams. Use interior columns and detailed woodwork strategically.

Economical historical details. If your house features a vintage style, maintain modern construction methods while using proportions and materials that are historically accurate.

Centrally located utilities. Centralize utilities to minimize the amount of ductwork and plumbing. Place the water heater and furnace at the center of the lower level to save considerable money on ductwork and plumbing runs.

Save on Materials

You might want granite countertops and marble floors, but if your budget dictates otherwise, take heart: Many alternatives to top-drawer materials offer the look and performance of more expensive materials at a bargain price. Careful material specing can save you significant money while giving you the look you want. Here are some areas to scrutinize for savings:

- *Flooring.* Carpet and vinyl flooring are lower-cost alternatives to hardwood, ceramic, and marble. And floors can be upgraded room-by-room later.

- *Windows.* Locally manufactured wood windows can often be found in the needed configurations and at a reduced price because they don't need to be shipped. If you plan to paint the window trim, consider vinyl windows instead of wood—they're less expensive and require lower maintenance. Consider energy costs as well as initial costs here; window-glazing options help with home energy efficiency. Make individual window selections based on the home's orientation to the sun.

- *Doors.* If you plan to paint interior doors, consider solid-core hardboard instead of solid wood. They're less expensive, take paint as well if not better than the wood doors, and have the same heft. Sliding glass doors are generally less expensive than French doors, and many designs look just as elegant.

- *Countertops.* Consider splurging with stone or marble on the island or other small counter area, then surround it with tile or basic color solid-surfacing countertops. Still too costly? Try a granite-look laminate with an edge trim.

- *Cabinetry.* You can imitate many designer looks with a creative arrangement of standard cabinets. Cherry-stained maple or poplar gives the look of more expensive cherry wood. Some top-of-the-line cabinet manufacturers offer mid-price lines with similar construction. Many lower-priced domestic appliances now incorporate the features and looks of European models.

Buy Now, Finish Later

If the house you envision is a bit of a stretch, concentrate on getting the basic shell of your home—the shape and size you want—then concentrate on the upgrades later. Doing so spreads the financial burden over time and keeps you from building a house that you'll soon outgrow and have to trade. In the long run, the buy-now, finish-later option is both less expensive and more convenient. It's also more affordable in the short run. The following offers advice on how to implement this strategy:

Leave room to grow. If you don't have to finish a space immediately, don't. Bonus rooms, basements, and extra bathrooms are the most logical "waiting" rooms. You can finish these spaces initially with inexpensive materials so they can serve a good purpose in the meantime. An extra bathroom, for instance, might do duty as a walk-in closet at first; a bonus room, as a walk-in attic storage area. If your plans include a finished basement, though, it's far easier and more cost-effective to rough-in plumbing for a lower-level bathroom and incorporate appropriate ceiling height and windows at the time you build.

Landscape slowly. Plan to spread this expense over several years. Find a designer who doesn't charge for a master plan. Gradually phase in the plan at your convenience. If your community requires that you have a lawn at outset, seed is a much less expensive option than sod. You can grow your own landscaping too. Buying small, inexpensive trees rather than large ones makes good financial sense.

Add moldings later. Although it's difficult to resist the beautiful finished look of molding, you can easily add trim detail later. Consider installing trim yourself at your leisure, saving even more money over professional installation. Or finish main level and master suite trim up front and leave second- and walk-out-level trim detail and upgrades for later.

Participate in a Home Show

If you're dead-set on building a house with upgrades and extras in place, there's an alternative to the build-now, finish-later strategy: If you live in an area that puts on an annual home show, express your willingness to participate to your builder, who might be willing to add upgrades to your home at a reduced fee. A builder will want to show high-quality work to the public and is often willing to invest in the property to a degree as well. Your finished show house might benefit from the following perks:

Interior design consultation: Free; estimated value $5,000.

Basement carpet: 80 percent discount.

Solid-core doors: Upgraded from hollow-core doors at no extra cost.

Upgrade window trim and crown molding: No extra cost.

5¼-inch baseboards: Upgrade from 3¼-inch baseboards at no extra cost.

Upgrade wood floors: $2,000 savings.

Special-finish faucets: Upgrade from standard finish at reduced cost.

Crown molding on kitchen cabinets: Added at no extra cost.

Higher-quality windows: Upgrade from standard ones at no extra cost.

25-year warranty asphalt shingles: Upgrade from 20-year warranty shingles at no extra cost.

Additional landscaping: Backyard sod and extra flowers and bushes at no extra cost.

Select paint colors for each room: Upgrade from single color throughout at no extra cost.

Get Financing Help

No matter what the price of your home, the first financial hurdle you'll face is the down payment. Then you must deal with the ongoing expense of a mortgage and taxes. Here are some options that may help you out:

Build in a Home Ownership Zone (HOZ). The U.S. Department of Housing and Urban Development provides seed money to revitalize older neighborhoods—many of which feature a convenient, close-to-downtown location. Benefits to homeowners can include down-payment assistance, tax abatements, and low-interest mortgages. To see whether an HOZ is currently under way in your area, visit www.hud.gov/hoz/hoz97.cfm.

Find out if you qualify for a VA or FHA loan. Veterans Administration (VA) loans, designed to help qualified veterans, and government-backed Federal Housing Administration (FHA) loans can be great deals, but both have restrictions. VA loans require a certain number of years in the armed services; FHA loans have preset spending limits determined by median prices in a region; and both require lender participation.

If you don't qualify for either type, check your state and local housing authority for programs available to individuals with higher incomes.

Look for down-payment help. Many nonprofit and public charity organizations have been created to assist buyers, regardless of their income. Between 1 and 5 percent down-payment assistance is provided through "gift funds" that do not have to be repaid.

These organizations usually require a fee or donation, which is typically paid by the seller, and they require the participation of local banks, real estate agents, and sellers. Examples of these organizations include: Home Buyers Assistance Foundation (www.hbaf.org), Consumer Credit Assistance, Inc. (www.mygiftmoney.org), and Down Payment Assistance Program (www.buyers-assistance.com).

Buy-It-Yourself It used to be that contractors could get most building materials, appliances, and accessories for far less than they were available retail—and choose from a far wider selection. The advent of large-volume home-center stores has changed all that. Contractors still get a discount, but often you can find the same or better products for less if you're willing to invest some research and shopping time. If your skills lean more toward organization and administration, play the role of buyer rather than let your contractor do it. Your savings will be greatest if you have several months to shop before you start building. You'll also need a place to store large items, such as in your current home's garage. Ask department and appliance stores when their "scratch and dent" sales are—you can sometimes save hundreds of dollars on appliances with almost imperceptible defects. Keep your eye on sale flyers in newspapers and look for going-out-of-business sales too. If you think of buying it yourself as a quest, you may even find it fun.

Be Your Own General Contractor

After you obtain an affordable house plan and have researched financing, there is yet another way to cut costs. If you're willing to take on the job, you can save approximately 10 percent on the construction of your new home by acting as your own general contractor.

The general contractor is the cornerstone of a quality building team. He or she coordinates the work of various specialty contractors, such as plumbers, electricians, and drywallers, and ensures that the work is inspected by the proper authorities. For the service, the general contractor typically charges a percentage of the cost of a home.

If you have the time, you can do the job yourself and save from 5 to 10 percent of the cost of your home. (General contractors charge from 10 percent to 20 percent of the cost of a house, but because you won't be a volume or repeat customer for building product suppliers, you can't expect to save the entire amount that a professional general contractor would charge.)

In deciding whether to take on the role, weigh the potential savings against the cost of your own time and effort. In the beginning, acting as a general contractor is a full-time job. Later, during construction, you can expect to spend approximately 10 hours a week visiting the site, responding to contractors' questions, and meeting with inspectors.

The first couple of weeks are typically the most labor-intensive. That's when you secure financing and review contractors' bids to select the right people for the job. Read the contracts thoroughly because the lowest price may not always be the best—or even the most cost-efficient—option.

Carefully research each contractor's experience and references. Make sure that most references are recent customers. Ask around local lumberyards or building associations to find out whether a contractor is financially responsible.

As a safety net, you might want to make contingency arrangements with a professional general contractor. That way, if you find yourself in over your head, you can hand off the project to someone you've already selected at a prearranged price.

Having a contingency plan also is a good way to help secure financing. Approach local banks that are familiar with the subcontractors with whom you plan to work. Larger national banks sometimes shy away from do-it-yourself projects. Approaching a financial institution with a well-organized written plan, however, will help impress lenders and improve your chances.

Finally, be flexible in working with contractors. A certain amount of detachment is helpful, and if your personal work experience includes project management or leading teams, you'll find your organizational skills a plus. Often couples split the general contractor functions; one does the organizing, for instance, and the other handles the paperwork.

Acting as a general contractor isn't for everyone, however, and even under the best circumstances, it has its drawbacks. If you're easily

---

Monitor the Job

Even if you choose to have your home professionally built from start to finish, you're more likely to get better quality if you monitor the work carefully. Building crews work fast, lots of subcontractors are involved, and mistakes and miscommunications can happen. So let your contractor know you'll be stopping by regularly to check progress and make sure everything's going according to plan.

Visit the house a few times when crews are at work, if possible, to introduce yourself and show them that you're interested in a quality job. It's easier to take a close look at things after hours, when you can pull out your tape measure, spread out your copy of the blueprints, and make sure everything is being built right.

Visit often during the process. Measure the foundation, check room dimensions, ensure walls are going up square and level, and see that windows, doors, fireplaces, and other major elements are being installed in the correct locations. Pay particular attention to unusual or custom features, which can be easily forgotten, especially by production-oriented crews. Check products as they arrive to make sure they're the ones you specified and that they've sustained no shipping damage.

If you do see something amiss, bring it to the attention of your architect, general contractor, or builder's representative right away, and recheck the item after it has been rectified.

excitable, poorly organized, have little patience in dealing with people, or find multitasking a challenge, leave the job to a pro.

Even if you're ideally suited to the task, you won't have the contacts, the know-how, and the draw of being able to offer repeat business that tends to attract the best subcontractors. As a small customer, you can expect to get low priority on the job lists of those you do hire.

Still, under the right circumstances, being your own general contractor can be not only a money-saving move but also a satisfying experience. When the job is completed, you'll have been a part of your home's creation every step of the way.

1 *If you're looking for the most square footage for the least money, build your home over a full basement. Insulated basements are energy-efficient, and if you stub in the wiring and plumbing and specify large windows with light wells, they can be warm, welcoming spaces. Best of all, you can finish them later, spreading out your costs.*

183

It's Easy Building Green

Green buildings are earth-friendly structures that are kind to the environment—and to their owners. They're designed to use natural, renewable materials that conserve energy and offer minimal disturbance to the building site. The home featured here is a stunning example and offers a wealth of lessons for anyone building a new home.

Sit lightly on the land. In addition to paying close attention to siting concerns (see "Siting Options," page 44), this homeowner left the field of clover and wildflowers that surrounds the home uncultivated and unmowed, *below*, providing habitat for wildlife and a beautiful, low-maintenance view. The driveway is gravel, and the road that meanders by the coastal Maine site is dirt, so there's no pavement to contribute to runoff problems. This house is also no bigger than it needs to be. The architect eliminated little-used but often-built spaces such as a guest

Alternative Building Materials

While sticks and bricks still dominate the new construction scene, a number of alternative materials—most of them "green," some new, some age-old—are gaining popularity. Most of these materials involve higher initial costs but promise energy savings and other benefits that should more than make up for the increased investment in the long run. If you see one that sounds attractive to you, look for a local builder who is familiar with the installation method; many require techniques that are unfamiliar to conventional stick-building contractors. Here's a quick glossary.

Adobe. A sun-dried mud brick commonly used in the southwestern United States. Its thick walls and high mass work well in evening out temperature extremes experienced in that region.

Autoclaved Aerated Concrete Blocks (AAC). These lightweight insulating blocks are made from concrete mixed with chemicals that cause them to rise like dough when heated. The mixture is pressure-cooked until its mass is about 80 percent air. Scandinavian countries have built with them for years. Relatively new in the U.S. market, they cost at least 20 percent more than traditional building materials but result in an unusually strong, solid, and energy-efficient building.

Engineered Wood. Thin layers of wood are glued together and microwave-cured to form large solid planks and beams. These offer more dimensional stability than traditional lumber—and consume fewer old-growth trees—for a 5–10 percent premium. Microwave-curing has essentially eliminated the outgassing problems of earlier products.

Insulated Concrete Forms. In this fast construction method, hollow foam forms are interlocked to form walls, then filled with concrete. The foam acts as insulation and the panels are usually reinforced with rebar, which adds to their structural stability. This method costs about 20 percent more than traditional means. The resulting houses are exceptionally well-insulated, have a virtually fireproof structure, and are extremely quiet inside. They're also low-maintenance, but their concrete-and-rebar walls can make them hard to add on to later.

Rammed Earth. Earth is molded into forms, then shaped into a conventional-looking structure. The process is similar to molding plaster of paris. No insulation is included, but it can be added in the middle of the forms if needed. Available only in certain regions during dry weather, the process is time-consuming, but the houses are solid, quiet, and environmentally friendly.

Rastra. This cement-based building system consists of recycled foam packing "peanuts" and a cement mixture. The components are combined to form large blocks. Rastra is stronger than conventional building methods, and buildings can be erected about 30 percent more quickly than with other masonry methods.

Straw Bale. Steel or timber frames are filled with straw, then the bales are stacked like bricks. The walls are thick—think of measurements in feet, not inches. The method offers exceptionally high R-values, is virtually fireproof (there's not enough air in the compressed straw to allow it to burn readily), and is very earth-friendly. Because straw is a fast-growing, renewable resource often available locally. Straw bale houses are usually covered with a stuccolike coating outside and plaster indoors that gives them a pleasingly rounded, adobelike look.

Steel Framing. Houses are framed with light-gauge steel studs instead of wood lumber, and they support heavier loads. More dimensionally stable, steel framing eliminates most drywall cracks. It's most suitable for mild climates, though, because steel readily conducts heat and cold, making poor insulation values relative to other alternative building methods (even relative to conventional wood framing).

Structural Insulation Panels (SIPs). Rigid panels of insulating foam are sandwiched between two sheets of plywood or other engineered wood product, such as Oriented Strand Board. The method was first used to make walk-in freezers and is extremely energy efficient. SIPs also use much less wood than conventional stud-built homes. Walls can be erected quickly; the panels are lightweight and arrive on-site filled with insulation. SIP houses are exceptionally sturdy.

---

room and a den. Doing so also eliminates the expense, material resources, and energy needed to heat and cool such spaces.

Help out the HVAC system. In the great-room, a fuel-efficient Orton fireplace, a variation on the time-tested Rumford design, fills a shallow firebox, *opposite above*. The design features a tall, wide opening that supplements the furnace. Large windows let in sunshine, yet their argon-filled thermal barriers are energy-efficient. Strategically placed doors and windows can be opened to let breezes sweep through the house. An open floor plan enables heated or cooled air to ciculate easily.

Use simple (or no) coatings. This house features water-based paints that have less odor and require less cleanup than oil-based coatings. The maple flooring in the master bedroom and throughout much of the house is treated with citrus-base oil for a light sheen that deepens over time. Most of the other exposed wood—the interior framing and ceiling members as well as the cedar shakes on the house exterior—was

left untreated to weather naturally.

Spend money where it counts. Custom kitchen cabinets cost more, but the home's modest-size galley kitchen, *above*, benefits from a custom design that maximizes efficiency. Paying extra for custom work can be worth the cost if doing so makes a smaller space more livable (and smaller custom spaces cost less than larger ones).

Skip the doors. An open floor plan uses fewer doors, saving material costs and the labor and time required to frame and hang them. Use other visual space dividers, such as changes in ceiling height or floor treatment, which allow the entire space to drink in the same sunlight, air, and views. For example, in the

children's bedrooms, *opposite below*, partitions instead of walls create a dormlike feeling and still provide privacy.

Leave surfaces exposed. The cost of drywall and the labor required to install it adds up quickly. This house leaves ceiling beams (such as those in the dining room, *top of page 188*) and recessed lighting exposed in several areas. Exposed framing members surround the stairway, which creates the illusion of more volume.

Use recycled, renewable, and natural products. This home's side entry features a floor of recycled materials (rubber embedded with

gas in high concentrations can be as dangerous as smoking multiple packs of cigarettes per day. Use these products and techniques outside and surrounding your house to get maximum health benefits.

• *Exterior-wall vapor barriers.* Use plastic sheeting in the wall cavity or an airtight drywall system to prevent moisture, pollutants, and drafts from entering the home.

• *Untreated kiln-dried lumber.* Avoid using treated lumber that contains chemicals that may outgas, or give off, volatile organic compounds (VOCs).

• *Native plants.* Planting indigenous shrubs, grasses, and flowers helps reduce the use of pesticides and fertilizers that are tracked into the home.

• *Healthy site.* If possible, select a radon-free location. For help, see www.epa.gov/iaq/radon/zonemap.html. Choose a site away from high-voltage power lines. Situate the house so that water drains away from the foundation.

• *Attic vents.* Vents at the roof eaves and ridge allow moist air to escape. Vent bath and kitchen exhausts to the outside, never to the attic.

• *Low-VOC sealants.* Use nontoxic, water-base adhesives and caulks around windows and perforations.

• *Opposing window placement.* Windows on opposites sides of a room create natural cross ventilation.

• *Mudroom.* This room isolates tracked-in dirt and moisture that can foster dust mites and mold.

• *Detached garage.* Stave off car exhaust and other vapors by building a separate garage. Or place an

neoprene chips) for a resilient, easy-to-clean surface, *left.* The exterior wood doors come from a company that buys wood from a conservation forest where a new tree is planted for every one that's harvested.

The kitchen floor linoleum is made from natural materials, bedrooms have carpets made from wool and sisal (a natural grasslike fiber), and maple wood covers the floors in most of the public areas of the house.

Healthy Surroundings

Breathe easier in your new home by improving air circulation, blocking mold growth, and reducing toxins with these building techniques and features:

Outside

An estimated 25 percent of Americans suffer from allergies, and radon attached garage downwind of the house, add an exhaust fan, and seal the walls.

• *Sealed foundation with ventilation.* Sealing walls and floors while providing controlled ventilation is most critical at the foundation level, where soil gases and moisture can easily seep into the home. One remedy is plastic sheeting layered under the slab. A pipe vented through the roof might be necessary for high-radon sites. Crawlspace vents and basement egress windows or mechanical exhaust fans prevent stale, moist air from accumulating.

Inside

The Environmental Protection Agency cites poor indoor air quality as the fourth-largest environmental threat. Indoor air may be 2 to 200 times more hazardous than outdoor air. Ironically, air quality in new homes can be particularly bad, due to the outgassing of paints and engineered wood products and new tight construction techniques designed to save energy. Use these products and techniques to improve the indoor air quality of your new home.

• *Low- or no-VOC paints.* Low-toxicity paints emit small amounts of chemical fumes and outgas quickly after application.

• *Air-filtration and ventilation system.* Combining ventilation and air-filtration systems ensures the cleanest air. An air-to-air heat exchanger brings fresh outside air in while recovering some of the heating and cooling energy of the spent outgoing air. Gas and medium-efficiency furnace filters installed at the return-air side help sift particles and vapors from the incoming air

sent via the heat exchanger.

• *Wood or metal window coverings.* Smooth-surface blinds are easier to keep clean. Choose flat-weave fabrics such as cotton and linen for treatments.

• *Sealed-combustion gas fireplaces.* Sometimes called "direct vent" fireplaces, these draw combustion air from the fire and vent it to the outside so no fumes or particulates taint indoor air. Do not confuse such fireplaces with so-called "vent-free" appliances, which can deplete indoor oxygen and usually require leaving a window open for ventilation.

• *Solid wood or UF-free products.* Many composite wood products such as pressed-wood furniture frames, plywood subfloors, and MDF cabinets contain urea formaldehyde (UF) which outgases VOCs.

• *Sealed metal ductwork.* Low-toxic mastic sealer or aluminum foil tape plugs leaks that can draw in unfiltered air. Your newly installed HVAC system should not be used to heat and dry the home during construction, when dust and insulation fragments can settle in the ducts. Even better: Install a radiant-floor heating system, which minimizes

airborne particulates.

• *Range hood.* A variable-speed range exhaust fan pulls smoke, odors, and airborne cooking grease outdoors.

• *Water-filtration system.* After testing your local water supply for contaminants, choose undercounter faucet and showerhead filters, or buy a whole-house system if needed.

• *Solid wood cabinets.* Cabinets made from pressed wood products often contain UF. A few suppliers offer low-emitting UF or UF-free composite board cabinets that can be used with solid wood doors. Check labels to see whether your cabinets are in compliance with American National Standards Institute criteria.

• *Hard-surface floors.* Hardwood and tile are easy to clean. Avoid wall-to-wall carpet because many brands outgas chemicals and the fibers trap dust and debris. Opt for area rugs, which can be removed for deep cleaning.

For more information on healthy homes, visit the American Lung Association website at www.health-house.org.

Outbuildings If you're building in the country—or just have a good-size lot—consider keeping your house compact to hold down up-front costs, then add bonus spaces later on in the form of outbuildings. A garage, for instance, can wait a couple of years, especially if you buy or build an inexpensive toolshed for yard and garden equipment. Along the way, you might find that a collection of outbuildings better suits your purposes than trying to cram everything into a single foundation. Outbuildings add to your property's interest and utility for comparatively little cost. Purpose-built architecture puts the features you want right where you need them and doesn't involve the disruption that home additions do. Buildings from potting sheds to pool houses, separate offices, studios, workshops, and more are possible. Look for books on outbuilding plans or ideas, or log on to the websites of companies that supply outbuildings in plan, material package, kit, or fully finished form.

Index

Index

lap, 27, 139, 142, 157
redwood, 90
shingles, 6, 134
stone, 14, 169
stucco, 110, 169
synthetic fieldstone/fiber
cement, 107
timber, 126
vertical boards/battens, 62
Siting options. *See also*
Location
bulldozing, clear-cutting,
45, 48
distance from street, 6
garage placement, 45, 48,
71, 111, 134, 151
Homesite Checklist, 43
house plans, 50–51
modifying drive, 131
natural landscape, 14, 184
to one side, 62, 110, 130
outdoor rooms, 45
planning, 48–49
rotating house direction,
11, 16, 44–45
on sloping lot, 106, 114,
115, 164, 168
on steep hillside, 90
using natural light, 28, 45,
48, 49, 51, 67, 71
Size of house, 50
Soil/water analysis, 44
Southern style, 156–159
Stairways
in back and front, 160
central, 78
curved, 11
exterior, 93, 119
newel post, 72
open, 171
rails/banisters, 75, 149
spiral, 89
switchback, 28
Storage
barrier-free closet, 171
in closets, 16, 37, 69, 137
by doors, 33, 114
for entertainment equip-

ment, 21
in hallway cabinets, 105
in lockers, 147
under stairways, 105
Structural Insulated Panels
(SIPs), 87
Studio, family, 146–147
Systems-built homes, 53, 94–97

T-V

Televisions, 98, 172–173. *See
also* Home theaters;
Media center
Texture
exterior, 7, 8, 14
interior, 83, 166
Theaters, home, 174–175
Themes, 46, 144, 164, 165
Tract development, 41
Traditional neighborhood devel-
opments (TNDs), 42
Traditional style, 66–69, 82–85
Traffic, 40, 43
Traffic flow, interior, 8, 13, 25,
142
Trial residence period, 40
Turrets/turret room, 6, 9
Two-story family style, 160–163
Universal Barrier-Free design,
170
Utilities, 43–44, 180
Victorian Gothic style, 6–9

W-Z

Wall treatments
beaded-board, 28, 62, 87
color/texture, 24, 31, 33,
37
metal, 118
natural materials, 17, 123
paneling, 77
plaster, 62
tall walls, 83
wallpaper, 23
Water/sewage access, 44
Websites

cost-of-living calculators,
58
job costs, 59
mortgage payment calcula-
tor, 58
outbuildings, 189
Wheelchair accessibility, 169,
170
Widow's walk, 6, 9
Window coverings
costs, 59
for privacy, 113
shutters, 144
for TV, 98
Window seat, 9, 25, 75, 84
Windows
awning, 93
basics/specifications, 103
budget-cutting materials,
180
clerestory, 12, 28, 90, 126,
134, 149
dormers, 27, 30, 31, 32,
114
glass block, 100, 147
interior, 27, 64, 80, 103
muntin, 69
and natural light, 51, 64,
103, 130
pass-through, 74, 77, 107
sidelights, 11, 12
skylight, 12, 119, 149, 169
specialty, 6, 7, 23, 30, 77,
82, 109, 134, 159
sun-diffusing glass, 119
transom, 12, 37, 100, 107,
131, 139, 155, 168
using best views, 51, 91,
102, 105
wells, 90, 152
Wiring, 52, 172–173
Wish list, 47
Woodwork, 35, 37, 78, 134,
164, 165
Wrightian style, 14–17, 90–93
Zones, interior, 98, 156
Zoning/regulations
future development, 44

house height, 90
Home ownership zone
(HOZ), 181
size, 51